The
frugal
keto
Cookbook

75 Flavor-Packed Recipes That Are
Easy on Your Budget

emily pierce

founder of Keto Copy

PAGE STREET
PUBLISHING CO.

PAGE STREET
PUBLISHING CO.

→ **for my sisters** ←

table of ➜ contents

→ introduction ←

I have battled my weight for almost my entire life, and my relationship with food was a painful struggle. It wasn't until I discovered a Ketogenic way of eating that I felt in control. Once I gave up sugar-filled sweets and carbohydrate-packed products, I felt real hunger and real satiety for the first time in my life. My relationship with food changed. It wasn't my appetite calling the shots anymore; it was me. I have lost 120 pounds since making the transition, and I have never looked back.

There are a lot of Keto products on the market that are really expensive, but Keto doesn't have to be pricy. In fact, when I first made the switch, I had the tightest budget I've ever had in my life. Don't let fear of high costs keep you from adopting a Ketogenic lifestyle. A frugal Keto approach is possible.

All you need to go Ketogenic is fresh, real food. I didn't join a club or a subscription service, and I didn't purchase anything at all except for fresh groceries. I carefully planned my shopping trips and planned my menus around what was on sale at my local market. I stocked up on pantry items that would allow me to make anything, and I do mean anything, myself. If there was a food that I missed from my Standard American Diet days I simply re-created it using Keto-friendly ingredients.

Once I had a well-rounded collection of items, I was off. I began creating my own recipes using only the ingredients available in my local grocery store—no fancy, expensive ingredients only available online. I wasted nothing. If I made something with egg whites, I would create a recipe using the egg yolks. I learned how to build flavors as I cooked, never wasting an opportunity to use what I had. I balanced my recipes carefully, trying to use easy, convenient measurements so they would be easy to double, triple or half. I made my own stocks and learned how to meal prep so I would always have a Keto option on hand. I learned how to make Keto affordable.

This book gathers all my experiences in one place. These recipes will take all the guesswork out of any frugal Keto menu. They are tried-and-true, delicious recipes that won't break the bank. Cooking your meals yourself, planning your menu around what is the best buy, stocking up on certain proteins when they go on sale, buying commonly used items in bulk—these are the keys to making the Keto diet affordable and sustainable, and I will discuss all of this and more in the coming pages! My goal is to prove that eating Keto on a budget isn't just doable, but enjoyable. So let's get started!

money-saving mains

Making the switch to a Ketogenic diet can feel expensive at first. You'll be stocking up on new pantry staples and fresh ingredients on that first grocery trip. If you haven't had a large meat budget in the past, it can seem like an enormous expense to load the fridge with protein-centered mains.

The good news is that some of the most flavorful and Keto-friendly cuts of meat are sometimes the most affordable. The super-tender Four-Hour Roast (page 13), for example, can be made with less expensive cuts. The Pancetta-Wrapped Chicken Breasts (page 28) give a fun twist to plain chicken breasts. I've also included some Ketofied versions of old favorites such as Carb-Cutting Eggplant Parmesan (page 31).

The methods you use to cook each of these meals will guarantee that you get outstanding texture and flavor for a low cost per serving. By doing your own prep, a bit of planning ahead, and never wasting an ingredient, these Keto mains will aid your wallet as well as your waist.

at-home fajitas

There's nothing like the sizzling platters of perfectly seasoned fajita meat that you get at a Mexican restaurant. This recipe re-creates all the flavors of a night out—at a fraction of the cost. We will be cooking the ingredients one after the other in the same pan so that each component of the dish adds layers and layers of flavor. Enjoy these on their own or wrapped in lettuce wraps or my Flexible Tortilla Wraps (page 99).

Serves 4 ←

Marinade
3 tbsp (45 ml) fresh lime juice
2 tbsp (30 ml) vegetable or olive oil
1 tbsp (15 ml) tamari
1 tsp onion powder
1 tsp garlic powder
1 tsp ground cumin
½ tsp chili powder
½ tsp cayenne pepper
½ tsp salt

Fajitas
2 lb (907 g) chicken breast, sliced into thin strips
3 tbsp (45 ml) vegetable or refined coconut oil, divided
1 medium yellow onion, thinly sliced
1 bell pepper, thinly sliced
1 tbsp (15 ml) lime juice

For Serving
Lime wedges
Fresh cilantro
Flexible Tortilla Wraps (page 99)
Guacamole
Sour cream

To make the marinade, in a small bowl, combine the lime juice, oil, tamari, onion powder, garlic powder, cumin, chili powder, cayenne and salt. Stir to combine.

Add the chicken, toss to coat it and let it marinate for at least 2 hours. Overnight is best!

To make the fajitas, in a 12-inch (30-cm) cast-iron pan, heat 1 tablespoon (15 ml) of oil and add half of the chicken strips. Cook the chicken over medium-high heat until it's cooked through, about 5 minutes. Remove the chicken and place it on a platter. Repeat with the other half of the chicken.

Pour 1 tablespoon (15 ml) of cooking oil in the hot pan and add the onion. Stir and cook it until the onion is golden brown, 5 to 10 minutes. Remove the onion and place it on a platter. Add the remaining oil to the pan along with the bell pepper and cook for 5 minutes, stirring frequently.

Turn the heat off and add 2 tablespoons (30 ml) of water plus the lime juice to the pan. Add the onion and chicken back to the pan and toss them together with the pepper. Make sure to scrape the bottom of the pan as you combine the ingredients to incorporate all of the flavors that have built up.

Place the fajitas back on the platter. Garnish with lime and cilantro and serve with tortillas, guacamole and sour cream.

the four-hour roast

I love a good roast. The best cuts of beef may not fit a frugal Keto budget, but this roasting method will yield a flavorful, tender roast in just four hours even if you're using the least expensive cuts. I make this on a day when I'm home and can turn it each hour. If that's not something you tend to do, this can be prepared in a slow cooker on the medium setting for eight hours. I use a package of fresh poultry herbs in this recipe. It's usually more economical to purchase fresh herbs in a variety assortment rather than one package of each herb—especially because a little goes a long way! Be sure to reserve the sage to make a side of delicious Caulimash (page 64).

Serves 4 to 6 ⬅

1 (½-oz [28-g]) package fresh poultry herbs (rosemary, thyme and sage)

1 tbsp (15 ml) vegetable or olive oil

3–4 lb (1.4–1.8 kg) chuck roast

1 quart (960 ml) beef broth

2 cloves garlic, crushed

½ white or yellow onion, chopped

½ tsp salt

1 lb (454 g) white button mushrooms, quartered (optional)

Preheat the oven to 350°F (177°C, or gas mark 4). Separate the sage from the poultry herbs and reserve it for another use, like my Caulimash (page 64).

Heat a large ovenproof saucepan over high heat. Add the oil and sear the roast for 2 to 3 minutes on each side, until the entire surface of the roast has a nice brown sear.

Reduce the heat to low and add the broth, poultry herbs, garlic, onion and salt. Cover the saucepan with a lid and place it in the oven for 4 hours, turning the roast every hour. For the last hour of roasting, add the washed mushrooms (if using). Spoon into bowls and enjoy!

lemon-pepper whole roast chicken

Roasting a whole chicken is one of the easiest, tastiest and most budget-friendly ways to prepare chicken. This recipe is simple yet delicious, and it will yield an incredibly flavorful, golden-brown dish. Seasoning this roast chicken simply also means it can be used in a multitude of ways as leftovers! Bake up a few at a time when they go on sale and break them down after cooling to have perfectly seasoned chicken on hand to use in other dishes. I frequently buy several whole chickens and store the cooked chicken meat in freezer bags. I use what's left to simmer up a batch of my Slow-Simmered Chicken Bone Broth (page 79)!

Serves 4 ←

1 (3–5-lb [1.4–2.3-kg]) whole roasting chicken

¼ cup (57 g) butter, melted

2 tsp (12 g) salt

Ground pepper

1 lemon, divided

Fresh sage or thyme (optional)

Bacon Blistered Green Beans (page 47) and Caulimash (page 64), for serving

Preheat the oven to 350°F (177°C, or gas mark 4).

Place the whole chicken, breast up, in a large roasting dish. Pat it dry and brush the entire surface of the chicken with butter. Evenly sprinkle the salt and pepper to taste over the entire chicken.

Cut the lemon in half; juice one half and reserve the other half. Add the juice to the bottom of the roasting pan. Place the juiced half of the lemon and the herbs (if using) inside the carcass.

Bake for 35 minutes per pound (454 g) of chicken. Check the chicken halfway through baking to ensure the surface isn't getting too browned. Cover it with foil if necessary. Remove the pan from the oven and allow the chicken to cool. Remove the lemon from inside the chicken. Serve with the reserved lemon and Bacon Blistered Green Beans and Caulimash on the side.

one-pan roast pork tenderloin

This one-pan dinner is ready in 45 minutes and is absolutely packed with flavor. This recipe uses one of the best do-it-all seasonings on the market: steak seasoning. A mixture of salt, pepper, dehydrated onion, garlic and other spices, it's a must-have pantry staple. Several varieties of steak seasoning are sold at bulk warehouse stores, which takes the price to pennies per serving. We will also build a delicious sauce in the same pan we roast the pork in to incorporate the flavors from roasting the tenderloin. This pork roast is delicious served with a leafy green or chunks of roasted cauliflower.

Serves 4 ⬅

1–2 lb (454–907 g) pork tenderloin
1 tbsp (8 g) steak seasoning
2 tbsp (30 ml) vegetable oil
1 cup (240 ml) heavy cream
1 tbsp (15 ml) stone-ground mustard

Preheat the oven to 350°F (177°C, or gas mark 4).

Pat the pork tenderloin dry and coat it in the steak seasoning. Heat a 12-inch (30-cm) cast-iron skillet over high heat. Pour in the oil and place the pork tenderloin in the pan. Let the pork sear for 5 minutes. Turn the pork tenderloin to the other side and roast it in the oven for 30 minutes.

Remove the pan from the oven and place it on the stove. Remove the pork from the pan and place it on a serving platter. Cover it loosely with foil. Turn the burner onto low heat and add the cream and mustard to the pan. Whisk the sauce together in the pan making sure to scrape up all the great flavor from the bottom of the pan. Heat the sauce over low heat for 3 to 5 minutes to allow the sauce to thicken.

Let the pork rest for 5 to 10 minutes, then slice it into 1-inch (2.5-cm) sections and serve it with the sauce.

chili-lime chicken burgers

Ground chicken is a super economical protein option. I buy it when it goes on sale and store it in the freezer in one-pound (454-g) packages. It is a great meat to have on hand because it can be seasoned and prepared in so many ways. You can use fresh ground chicken or turkey to make these burgers and then store them in the freezer for meal prep. Just transfer them to the fridge the night before you grill them up!

Serves 8 ⇐

2 lb (907 g) ground chicken or turkey

2 tsp (10 ml) lime juice

1 egg

½ cup (40 g) ground pork rinds

2 tsp (4 g) chili powder

½ tsp onion powder

½ tsp garlic powder

½ tsp salt

¼ tsp ground pepper (optional)

You Can Have Buns Again Hamburger Buns (page 105)

Fresh cilantro (optional)

Salsa, for serving

Lettuce, for serving

Crispy Parmesan Chips (page 122) or Guacamole with Pepperoni Chips (page 134), for serving

In a large mixing bowl, combine the ground chicken, lime juice and egg.

In a separate small bowl, combine the pork rinds, chili powder, onion powder, garlic powder, salt and pepper (if using). Stir the seasonings to combine them and then add them to the meat mixture.

Knead the mixture together with your hands until it is well combined. Form 8 patties. Cook the burgers, 2 or 3 at a time, in a large skillet over medium heat. The burgers will take 5 to 6 minutes per side to cook through.

Serve the burgers on buns with cilantro (if using), salsa and lettuce. I love to serve these with Crispy Parmesan Chips or Guacamole with Pepperoni Chips on the side.

black and blue burger

This blackening seasoning is a perfect complement to fish or chicken or in this, a burger finished with blue cheese. This recipe uses only about half of the mixture to dust the burgers; I store my leftover blackening seasoning in a small glass jar. Making my own seasoning mixes saves money, and it dramatically reduces the carbohydrate count when compared to store-bought blackening seasoning.

Makes 6 burgers

Blackening Seasoning
1 tbsp (7 g) smoked paprika
1 tsp onion powder
1 tsp garlic powder
1 tsp chili powder
½ tsp cayenne pepper
½ tsp thyme
½ tsp salt

Burgers
2 lb (907 g) ground beef
1 tbsp (30 ml) vegetable oil
1 cup (135 g) blue cheese

Serving Options
You Can Have Buns Again
Hamburger Buns (page 105)
Sliced red onion
Lettuce

Preheat the oven to 375°F (190°C, or gas mark 5) and place a rack at the top.

To make the seasoning, combine the paprika, onion powder, garlic powder, chili powder, cayenne, thyme and salt in a small bowl. Set aside.

To make the burgers, place the ground beef in a large mixing bowl and form 6 patties. Coat the surface of each burger in blackening seasoning. Heat the oil in a cast-iron pan over medium heat and sear the burgers for 5 minutes. Flip the burgers and sear them for 3 minutes more.

Remove the burgers from the pan and place them on a baking sheet. Top each burger with one-sixth of the blue cheese. Place the baking sheet in the oven for 10 minutes. Remove the baking sheet from the oven and lightly cover it with foil to keep the burgers warm until ready to serve.

Enjoy on a bun or with sliced red onion wrapped in lettuce.

scanty shrimp scampi

Seafood tends to be an expensive ingredient. One pretty reliable exception to this rule is frozen shrimp. You can usually find one-pound (454-g) bags at the grocery store for a pretty reasonable price! I stock up when they are on sale and also make this dish with fresh shrimp when they are on special. To defrost a bag of frozen shrimp, I simply place the shrimp in a bowl of room-temperature water for about 30 minutes. This is a delicious dish on its own or served over low-carb pasta or zucchini noodles.

Serves 2 ⬅

1 tbsp (15 ml) olive oil

2 tbsp (28 g) butter

1 tbsp (9 g) finely chopped garlic

1 (1-lb [454-g]) bag of medium or small shrimp, defrosted

Juice of ½ lemon

¼ cup (15 g) chopped fresh parsley

½ tsp salt

¼ cup (25 g) grated Parmesan cheese (optional)

Zucchini noodles or your favorite low-carb pasta

Heat a medium skillet over medium heat. Combine the olive oil, butter and garlic in the skillet. Sauté the garlic for about 1 minute until softened.

Cook the shrimp in two batches: Add half of the shrimp to the skillet. Stir to coat each shrimp and cook them for about 4 minutes per side. Remove the shrimp and place them in a bowl. Repeat the process with the remainder of the shrimp.

Turn the heat off and add the first batch of shrimp back into the skillet. Pour in the lemon juice and add the parsley. Sprinkle with salt and stir. Top with Parmesan (if using). Serve over zucchini noodles or pasta.

savory turmeric spiced chicken

Sometimes you just need a meal that's rich and warm. The flavors in this savory stew come together beautifully in a delicious creamy sauce using ingredients you probably already have in your pantry. Ready in about 45 minutes, this is a real comfort food recipe.

Serves 4 ⬅

4 tbsp (57 g) butter
2 lb (907 g) chicken breast, cut into 1-inch (2.5-cm) cubes
1 cup (240 ml) heavy cream
1 tbsp (16 g) tomato paste
1 tbsp (9 g) turmeric
1 tsp salt
1 tsp garlic powder
1 tsp onion powder
½ tsp cumin
½ tsp smoked paprika
½ tsp ground ginger
¼ tsp ground cinnamon
Chopped fresh cilantro, for garnish (optional)

Add the butter to a large saucepan over medium-high heat. Once the butter is melted and starts to bubble, add half of the chicken and sear it on all sides until the outside is cooked, about 5 minutes. Remove the cooked chicken to a platter and repeat with the second half of the chicken. Then add the first half of the chicken back into the pan with the second half and reduce the heat to medium.

Add the heavy cream and the tomato paste. Stir to combine and let the mixture come to a simmer. Add the turmeric, salt, garlic powder, onion powder, cumin, smoked paprika, ginger and cinnamon. Stir all of the ingredients together for several minutes while the mixture continues to simmer. Reduce the heat to low and cook for 15 minutes, covered. Stir the mixture frequently as it simmers.

After 15 minutes, uncover the dish and check the sauce for thickness. If the sauce is still pretty thin, simmer uncovered for an additional 15 minutes. If the sauce seems thick and rich, simmer for an additional 15 minutes covered.

Serve the chicken immediately, preferably over Caulimash (page 64). Sprinkle with chopped fresh cilantro before serving.

steak with blue cheese butter

Steaks are my favorite thing to throw on the grill in the summer. I also like eating steaks at home, all year round. To get the most bang for my buck at the grocery store, I buy family packs of steaks and freeze what I don't cook up that night. This indoor cooking technique adds a bonus of rich flavor that can sometimes be missing after a steak has been frozen. These steaks will come out of the oven sizzling and ready to serve.

Serves 4 ←

½ cup (68 g) crumbled blue cheese
½ cup (114 g) butter, softened
½ tsp Worcestershire sauce
¼ tsp garlic powder
1 tsp vegetable or canola oil
2 (8-oz [226-g]) strip steaks
Rosemary Garlic Radishes (page 51)

Preheat the oven to 350°F (177°C, or gas mark 4) and place a rack at the top.

Place the blue cheese and the butter in a mixing bowl. Stir to combine. Mix in the Worcestershire sauce and garlic powder. You will have a thick, paste-like mixture. Set aside.

Heat a large, ovenproof skillet over medium-high heat. Add the oil to the hot skillet. Pat the steaks dry and place them in the skillet. Let the steaks sear for 5 minutes. Turn the steaks and top each with half of the blue cheese mixture. Let the steaks sear for 3 minutes.

Place the skillet in the oven for 5 to 10 minutes, depending on how well you like your steaks done. Cook them for 5 minutes for a medium-rare steak and up to 10 minutes for a well-done steak. Serve with the garlic radishes.

flank steak with chimichurri

I used to absolutely love flank steak smothered in steak sauce. The problem there is that most steak sauces are absolutely packed with unnecessary carbohydrates. Using flank, hanger or skirt steak in this recipe will yield super tasty results with far fewer carbs. Marinate for at least two hours for best results—overnight is even better!

Serves 4

Marinated Flank Steak
2 tbsp (30 ml) tamari

2 tbsp (30 ml) red wine vinegar

2 cloves garlic

4 tbsp (60 ml) olive oil, divided

Pinch of salt and ground pepper

2 tbsp (8 g) chopped fresh parsley

2 lb (907 g) flank steak

Chimichurri
2 cloves garlic

1 cup (60 g) chopped fresh parsley

1 tbsp (15 ml) lime juice

2 tbsp (30 ml) red wine vinegar

¼ cup (60 ml) olive oil

1 tsp oregano

To prepare the steak, in a covered dish or ziplock bag, combine the tamari, vinegar, garlic, 2 tablespoons (30 ml) of oil, salt, pepper and parsley. Add the steak and allow it to marinate in the fridge for at least 2 hours.

While the steak is marinating, make the chimichurri. Combine the garlic, parsley, lime juice and vinegar in a food processor or blender. Pulse the mixture until the parsley has been chopped into very small pieces. Place the mixture in a medium bowl and add the olive oil and oregano. Stir gently to combine. Cover and place the bowl in the fridge until ready to serve.

To make the steak, heat a cast-iron or ovenproof skillet over medium-high heat with 2 tablespoons (30 ml) of oil. Remove the steak from the marinade and pat dry. Place the steak in the pan and sear for 5 minutes. Flip the steak and sear the other side for 5 minutes.

Remove the pan from the heat and cover it loosely with foil. Let the steak rest for at least 10 minutes or until ready to serve. Slice the steak into thin strips across the grain and serve with the chimichurri sauce.

pancetta-wrapped chicken breasts

Chicken breasts are a staple in my house. Family packs tend to go on sale frequently in my area and when they do, I stock up. Some preparations of chicken breasts tend to be repetitive and boring. This recipe for pancetta-wrapped, cheese-filled chicken breasts is not! Each breast is stuffed with herbed Boursin cheese, wrapped in pancetta and coated in crispy pork rind crumbs. It really is an outstanding main dish. The pancetta and ground pork rinds supply the perfect amount of salt and the cheese is a delicious, melty and flavorful surprise. I like to serve these chicken breasts with creamed spinach (page 133).

Serves 4 to 8 (6 to 8 ounces of chicken per serving) ←

4 chicken breasts
1 wheel Boursin cheese
2 eggs
12 slices pancetta
2 cups (160 g) ground pork rinds

Preheat the oven to 375°F (190°C, or gas mark 5). Line a baking sheet with parchment paper.

Slice each chicken breast in half being careful not to cut all the way through. We want to leave one side attached so we have a pouch. Fill each chicken breast with one-quarter of a wheel of Boursin cheese.

Crack the eggs into a bowl and whisk them. Drag the pancetta through the egg and wrap it around the chicken breast. Each breast usually takes 2 to 3 slices of pancetta to cover completely. Make sure you have covered the cut end of the chicken with pancetta.

Roll the wrapped chicken breast in the pork rinds and place it on the baking sheet. Bake for 45 minutes. Allow the chicken to cool for 10 minutes before slicing.

note: For a thicker crust, coat the chicken once with pork rind breadcrumbs and place it in the refrigerator for 30 minutes. Roll the chicken breasts in egg and then pork rinds again before baking.

carb-cutting eggplant parmesan

Most Italian dishes are heavy on pasta and carbohydrates. Not this version of eggplant Parmesan! We substitute a mixture of crushed pork rinds, seasoning and Parmesan cheese for traditional breadcrumbs. After baking the eggplant slices, you can serve this over zucchini noodles or your favorite low-carb noodle. I enjoy broiling them up one at a time as a small plate—this method keeps the eggplant slices crispy.

Serves 4

1 large eggplant
1 egg
2 cups (160 g) ground pork rinds
¼ cup (25 g) Parmesan cheese
1 tsp Italian seasoning
1 cup (240 ml) low-carb marinara
1 cup (112 g) shredded mozzarella or provolone cheese

Preheat the oven to 350°F (177°C, or gas mark 4) and place a rack at the top. Line a baking sheet with parchment paper.

Slice the eggplant into ¼- to ½-inch (6-mm to 1-cm) slices. Grab two dishes, one for the egg, one for the seasoned pork rind crumbs. I like to use glass pie plates. Scramble the egg and add it to one plate. Mix together the pork rinds, Parmesan cheese and Italian seasoning and add it to the other plate.

Take one slice of eggplant and place it in the egg mixture. Make sure to cover both sides in egg. Allow any excess to drip off and then place the eggplant in the seasoned "crumb" mixture. Coat both sides and place the eggplant on the baking sheet. Bake for 30 to 40 minutes. The eggplant is done when it has softened and the coating is golden brown.

You can prepare all of the eggplant cutlets together, layered with sauce and cheese like a traditional presentation, or serve individually as small plates. I enjoy dividing the sauce among the eggplant slices, right on the same baking dish, and then topping with cheese. Place the baking sheet back in the oven for 15 minutes. When the eggplant parmesan is done cooking, spoon it onto a plate and enjoy!

egg noodle lasagna

Lasagna is a comfort classic that I have never stopped craving. You don't have to give it up when you adopt a Ketogenic diet. There are plenty of swaps out there for the carbohydrate-heavy pasta noodles, but I've never found that those swaps really hit the spot. The noodles that we will make to support layers of delicious seasoned ricotta cheese, rich meat sauce and melty mozzarella are a great low-carb substitution. The noodles can be made in advance and stored in an airtight bag before using, or you can bake up a batch while you simmer your meat sauce to perfection.

Serves 4 to 6 ⬅

Sauce
1 lb (454 g) ground beef
2 cups (480 ml) low-carb tomato sauce
1 tbsp (16 g) tomato paste
1 tsp garlic powder
1 tsp onion powder
½ tsp Italian seasoning
1 tsp sweetener, such as Lakanto

Noodles
2 cups (224 g) shredded mozzarella cheese
4 egg yolks
½ cup (52 g) almond flour
½ tsp baking powder
¼ tsp garlic powder
¼ tsp xanthan gum
1 tsp vegetable oil

Preheat the oven to 350°F (177°C, or gas mark 4).

To make the sauce, in a large saucepan, brown the ground beef over medium-high heat for 8 to 10 minutes. Once cooked, drain off any excess moisture. Reduce the heat to medium-low and add the tomato sauce, tomato paste, garlic powder, onion powder, Italian seasoning and sweetener. Stir it together until it comes up to a simmer. Reduce the heat to low and cover. Allow the sauce to simmer for 10 to 15 minutes while you prepare the "noodles."

To make the noodles, place the mozzarella in a microwave-safe bowl and microwave in 30-second bursts, stirring each time, until it's melted. Add the egg yolks and stir to combine. In a separate bowl, combine the almond flour, baking powder, garlic powder and xanthan gum. Whisk the dry ingredients together and then add them to the cheese mixture. Stir together until well combined. The mixture will be sticky.

Drizzle the vegetable oil onto a piece of parchment. Place another piece of parchment on top of the oiled parchment. This will coat both pieces of parchment with oil. Roll the dough out between the pieces of parchment until it's the size of a half sheet baking sheet. The noodle layer will be thin. Set it aside and make the ricotta.

Ricotta

8 oz (226 g) full-fat ricotta
cheese
1 egg
¼ tsp garlic powder
¼ tsp salt

Lasagna

2 cups (224 g) shredded
mozzarella cheese
Pizza Shop Garlic Knots
(page 95)

To make the ricotta, in a medium mixing bowl, combine the ricotta cheese, egg, garlic powder and salt. Stir it well until it is completely incorporated.

To make the lasagna, pour ½ cup (120 ml) of the meat sauce into the bottom of a large lasagna pan. Cut the noodle sheet in half and place the first half over the sauce. Spoon half of the ricotta mixture over the noodle layer. Top the ricotta with half of the meat sauce and top with 1 cup (112 g) of shredded mozzarella. Place the second half of the noodle sheet on top of the mozzarella. Spoon the second half of the ricotta mixture over the noodle. Top with the remaining meat sauce and remaining shredded mozzarella cheese.

Cover with foil and bake for 45 minutes. Remove the foil cover and bake for 10 to 15 minutes, until the cheese is browned and bubbly on top. Allow the lasagna to cool for at least 10 minutes before serving with garlic knots.

savory asian lettuce wraps

I used to frequent a popular restaurant in my area, famous for their lettuce-wrapped spiced pork. I thought that by skipping the noodles I was avoiding the most carb-heavy dishes. I was wrong! The sauce that the ground pork was simmered in was absolutely filled with sugar. Not wanting to miss out on the delicious flavors of this dish, I set out to re-create this restaurant favorite. By swapping out the sugar-packed sauce with just the right seasonings and some sugar-free syrup, these lettuce wraps fit beautifully into a low-carb diet.

Serves 4

2 tbsp (30 ml) vegetable or refined coconut oil

1 small yellow or white onion, chopped

1 tbsp (9 g) finely chopped garlic

2 ribs celery, finely chopped

2 lb (907 g) ground chicken, turkey or pork

¼ cup (60 ml) rice vinegar

¼ cup (60 ml) tamari

1 tbsp (15 ml) sesame oil

1 tsp Chinese five-spice mix

2 tbsp (30 ml) sugar-free maple syrup

¼ cup (12 g) sliced green onions, plus more to garnish

Ground pepper

Bibb or butter lettuce leaves

Sesame seeds (optional)

Sriracha (optional)

Warm the oil in a large skillet over medium heat. Add the onion, garlic and celery. Cook for 3 to 5 minutes, stirring frequently. Add the ground chicken. Cook for 5 to 10 minutes, stirring and breaking up the meat.

After the chicken is cooked through, reduce the heat to low and add the vinegar, tamari, sesame oil, Chinese five-spice and sugar-free maple syrup. Simmer this mixture together for 5 to 10 minutes until most of the moisture has absorbed. Turn off the heat.

Add the green onions, season to taste with pepper and stir to combine well. Serve this on lettuce leaves with additional green onions, pepper, and sesame seeds and with Sriracha drizzled on top (if using).

note: This recipe can easily be cut in half with 1 pound (454 g) of ground chicken to serve two people.

tuscan chicken skillet

I love a recipe that comes together in one pan. It cuts down on dishes, and it gives an opportunity to build flavors layer by layer. This recipe incorporates the flavors of sun-dried tomatoes in a way that allows for a little to go a really long way. Adding greens in the last few minutes of cooking makes this a delicious complete meal which is frugal in concept but certainly not in flavor.

Serves 4 ←

2 tbsp (30 ml) olive oil

2 large chicken breasts

¼ cup (40 g) chopped yellow onion

2 cloves garlic, chopped

¼ cup (60 ml) chicken stock

1 cup (240 ml) heavy cream

½ cup (120 ml) low-carb tomato sauce

⅓ cup (33 g) grated Parmesan cheese

¼ cup (14 g) chopped sun-dried tomatoes, rehydrated or packed in oil

½ tsp salt

Ground pepper

½ tsp dried basil

½ tsp dried oregano

4 cups (268 g) chopped kale

Preheat the oven to 350°F (177°C, or gas mark 4).

Heat a large ovenproof skillet over medium heat and pour in the olive oil. Pat dry the chicken breasts and sear them in the skillet for 5 to 10 minutes per side. Remove the chicken from the pan and set it aside on a plate.

Add the onion to the pan. Sauté over medium heat until softened, about 5 minutes. Add the garlic and stir for 2 to 3 minutes until fragrant. Lower the heat to low or simmer. Pour the chicken stock into the pan and stir the onion and garlic, making sure to scrape the bottom of the pan to pick up all of the flavors. Add the heavy cream, tomato sauce, Parmesan cheese, sun-dried tomatoes, salt, pepper, basil and oregano. Continue to stir the sauce over low heat until the mixture begins to bubble.

Add the chicken breasts to the pan, cover it and place it in the oven. Bake for 30 minutes. Remove the pan from the oven, uncover it and fold in the kale. Cover and place it back in the oven for 10 minutes. Remove from the oven and enjoy hot!

spicy sausage with collards

This delicious dish comes together quickly and all in one pan! I love the way the heavy cream balances out the spice from the red pepper flakes. You can play with the amount of flakes to control the level of heat. The flavors build in the pan as we cook and then meld together just beautifully once the dish is covered and baked for the last 30 minutes. This can be served right from the pan!

Serves 4 ←

1 tbsp (30 ml) vegetable oil
2 lb (907 g) spicy sausage, Andouille or spicy Italian
¼ cup (40 g) chopped yellow onion
1 clove garlic, chopped
½ cup (120 ml) chicken broth or stock
1 cup (240 ml) heavy cream
1 tbsp (4 g) red pepper flakes
½ tsp salt
¼ tsp dried thyme
¼ tsp ground pepper
2 cups (134 g) chopped collard or mustard greens

Preheat the oven to 350°F (177°C, or gas mark 4).

Heat a large ovenproof pan over medium heat. Pour in the oil and add the sausage. Sear the sausage for 5 minutes and then turn. Sear the other side for 5 minutes, then remove the sausage from the pan.

Add the onion and sauté it for 3 to 5 minutes until softened. Add the garlic and cook for about 1 minute until fragrant. Add the broth and heavy cream to the pan. Lower the heat to medium and stir the sauce with a wooden spoon or spatula until well combined, making sure to scrape any bits of browning on the bottom of the pan. Add the red pepper flakes, salt, thyme and pepper. Stir to combine.

Place the sausages back into the pan and cover with the greens. Cover the pan and bake for 30 minutes. Serve the sausage on a plate with the collard greens and sauce spooned on top.

fresh walnut pesto pasta

Pesto is an extremely flavorful and Keto-friendly sauce. Most recipes for pesto call for pine nuts, an extremely expensive ingredient. This recipe swaps out the costly pine nuts for a much more budget-friendly nut, the walnut. When fresh basil is in season, it's also an extremely affordable ingredient. By toasting the walnuts for only a few minutes, we will have a delicious, rich substitution for the pine nuts. This sauce is amazing served over grilled chicken breast or spooned over fresh zucchini noodles. To make this sauce even more frugal, you can substitute half of the basil with fresh baby spinach.

Serves 4 ←

1 cup (117 g) walnuts, chopped
2 cloves garlic
½ cup (120 ml) light olive oil
2 cups (80 g) fresh basil
½ cup (50 g) plus 1 tbsp (8 g) grated Parmesan cheese
¼ cup (60 ml) extra virgin olive oil
¼ tsp salt (optional)
Zucchini noodles, cooked

Preheat the oven to 325°F (163°C, or gas mark 3).

Spread the walnuts over a small baking sheet and toast them dry in the oven for 5 to 10 minutes. The walnuts will be fragrant and slightly golden brown.

Place the walnuts in a food processor or blender along with the garlic. Pulse the mixture until the nuts are finely ground but not so much that they begin to make a paste. Pour in the light olive oil and add the fresh basil. Pulse a few times and then scrape down the sides of the blender or food processor. Pulse a few more times. Repeat this process until the pesto mixture has an evenly chopped consistency.

Pour the mixture into a medium mixing bowl and add the Parmesan cheese. Stir the mixture together and add the extra virgin olive oil, 1 tablespoon (15 ml) at a time until you have a nice thick, but spoonable mixture. Taste for salt and add it if needed. Parmesan is sometimes salty enough on its own for this dish, so taste first. Add the zucchini noodles to the sauce, stirring until they're warmed through, then divide the pasta equally among 4 plates to serve. This is great served over chicken and zoodles.

small plates, sides and starters

Small, shareable plates have always been one of my favorite ways to dine. I like tasting a bit of everything rather than committing to one dish. The way we eat and entertain has changed as well. Sometimes setting out small plates and starters is a perfect, fun dinner!

This chapter is full of sides you can prepare to accompany a main, such as the seasoned Caulimash (page 64) or Bacon Blistered Green Beans (page 47). It also has several small plate items, such as delicious Cheesy Baked Zucchini Fritters (page 63) and Superbowl Stuffed Mushroom Caps (page 44), that would please any crowd. However you choose to enjoy these dishes, they are easy to prepare, budget-friendly and fit perfectly into a low-carb lifestyle.

superbowl stuffed mushroom caps

When I first went Keto, one of the first foods I really started to miss were party foods. And for me, stuffed mushroom caps have always been party food. During Thanksgiving and Christmas and the big football game, we always had stuffed mushrooms. Finger foods! Swapping out traditional breadcrumbs for grated Parmesan cheese and ground pork rinds is an easy way to make an old favorite into a new favorite. For this recipe you will want to buy two 8-ounce (226-g) packages of mushrooms, or buy one 1-pound (454-g) package and select the twelve prettiest, most similarly sized caps.

Makes 12 mushroom caps ⬅

12 mushrooms
8 oz (226 g) uncooked pork sausage
½ tsp ground sage
¼ tsp garlic powder
¼ tsp salt
¼ cup (25 g) plus 2 tbsp (12 g) grated Parmesan cheese, divided
¼ cup (20 g) ground pork rinds

Preheat the oven to 350°F (177°C, or gas mark 4) and place a rack in the middle.

Clean the mushrooms and remove their stems. If any have a really tight stem, cut around the hole to enlarge the surface for stuffing.

Combine the sausage, sage, garlic powder, salt, ¼ cup (25 g) of Parmesan and the pork rinds in a bowl. Mix well with your hands.

Place the mushrooms in a medium baking dish and divide the stuffing equally between the mushrooms. Sprinkle the tops with the 2 tablespoons (12 g) of Parmesan and bake for 20 to 25 minutes. I checked at 25 minutes to make sure the sausage had cooked through by cutting it in half.

These are best served hot. This recipe can be made a day ahead of time and popped in the oven just before serving. It also reheats well in the microwave the next day. Make sure to store any leftovers in an airtight container in the fridge.

bacon blistered green beans

Green beans are an affordable and Keto-friendly vegetable to buy fresh. There are numerous ways to prepare green beans, but this method, which uses just three simple ingredients, is by far my favorite. Whenever I make bacon, I reserve the fat to use in dishes like this one—it's a super frugal way to add an incredible amount of flavor.

Serves 4

2 tbsp (28 g) bacon fat
1 lb (454 g) green beans, trimmed
¼ tsp salt

Heat a heavy saucepan over medium-high heat. Melt the bacon fat in the pan and fry the green beans in the bacon fat for 2 to 3 minutes before stirring. The hot bacon fat will cook the green beans and impart a great charred flavor.

Stir the green beans and allow them to cook for 10 minutes. Reduce the heat to medium-low, sprinkle the salt over the green beans and cover the pan with a lid. The steam will continue to soften and cook the green beans. Cook with the lid on for 5 minutes for an al dente green bean, 10 minutes for a softer texture. Serve alongside any money-saving main.

cookout faux-tato salad

A summer barbecue is usually full of not-so-Keto-friendly foods. Even the meat mains can be tricky if they are coated with sugary sauces. This recipe for faux-tato salad is a great stand-in for a traditional potato salad. This recipe is also a great way to use up any stalks of cauliflower left over from making cauliflower rice, and it's perfect served alongside Chili-Lime Chicken Burgers (page 18) or Black and Blue Burgers (page 21).

Serves 4 ⬅

1 head of cauliflower, plus any stems if available
¼ cup (40 g) chopped yellow onion
2 ribs celery, chopped
¼ cup (60 ml) mayo
1 tbsp (15 ml) mustard
½ tsp salt

Chop the cauliflower into small chunks, about ½ inch (1 cm) across. Place the cauliflower chunks in a large, microwave-safe bowl along with 3 tablespoons (45 ml) of water. Cover the bowl and microwave for 5 minutes.

Remove the cauliflower and uncover the bowl to check for doneness, being careful to avoid the steam. Slide a knife into one of the cubes of cauliflower. If it slides in easily it's ready, if not, microwave for 2 to 3 minutes more.

In a medium bowl, combine the onion, celery, mayo, mustard and salt. Stir to combine. Once the cauliflower has cooled, pour the sauce over the cauliflower and fold it together with a spatula. Once well combined, cover the bowl with plastic wrap and refrigerate for at least 1 hour before serving.

tasty roasted cauliflower steaks

Cauliflower can be a substitute for just about anything. Add butter and sour cream to cooked cauliflower and you get a lovely mashed potato substitute. Roast and simmer it in chicken broth and you will get a delicious soup. Sometimes I just want my cauliflower to be a cauliflower!

Roasting is my favorite way to prepare this do-it-all veggie. The flavors concentrate and you get a lovely golden-brown finish. Cutting cauliflower into evenly sliced steaks ensures that each piece cooks evenly. Roasting the cauliflower using this technique allows the entire face of the cauliflower steak to brown up just beautifully. It makes such a lovely presentation on the plate. I love serving these steaks as a side to my One-Pan Roast Pork Tenderloin (page 17). By seasoning these steaks simply, the leftovers can be used in a variety of dishes, such as my Roasted Cauliflower Soup (page 83)!

Serves 4 to 6 ⬅

1 head of cauliflower
2 tbsp (30 ml) olive oil
1 tbsp (14 g) butter, melted
½ tsp salt
Ground pepper

Preheat the oven to 375°F (190°C, or gas mark 5) and place a rack in the middle. Line a baking sheet with parchment paper.

Slice 1-inch (2.5-cm)-thick steaks through the head of cauliflower straight down, leaving the stem intact. Place the steaks on the baking sheet.

Brush each cauliflower steak with olive oil and melted butter, then sprinkle them with salt and pepper. Roast in the oven for 35 to 45 minutes. Your cauliflower steaks will be done when they are golden brown and you can slide a knife through one with little resistance.

Serve these alongside any protein-based main, such as One-Pan Roast Pork Tenderloin (page 17).

rosemary garlic radishes

This recipe for garlic-roasted rosemary radishes is a perfect sub for roasted new potatoes. It's bright and colorful and delicious. Roasting radishes brings out a whole different flavor profile versus eating them raw. They easily absorb the flavors of whatever they are cooked with. To bring out even more flavor, this dish calls for a browned butter sauce. It's a simple addition at the end of cooking and takes these radishes over the top. This is delicious served alongside The Four-Hour Roast (page 13).

Serves 4 ⬅

1 bunch radishes, sliced (about 2 cups [232 g])
2 tbsp (30 ml) olive oil
¼ cup (57 g) butter
2 cloves garlic, chopped
¼ tsp salt
¼ tsp thyme
½ tsp rosemary
Ground pepper
Fresh parsley (optional)

Preheat the oven to 375°F (190°C, or gas mark 5).

In a medium bowl, toss the radishes in the olive oil. Bake for 30 minutes in a covered baking dish. Remove the radishes from the oven and toss. Place the radishes back in the oven, uncovered, for 15 minutes.

In a small saucepan, melt the butter over medium-low heat. Allow the butter to brown slightly. This should take 3 to 5 minutes. Turn off the heat as soon as the butter reaches a golden-brown color and has achieved a slightly nutty aroma. Move the saucepan to a cool burner. Add the garlic, salt, thyme and rosemary. Stir the herbs into the browned butter.

Remove the radishes from the oven and add the garlic-butter mixture to the baking dish. Stir to coat the radishes evenly. Garnish with the ground pepper and fresh parsley (if using).

hearty bacon mac and cheese

There really is no better comfort food than macaroni and cheese. I have given up the pasta—but not the craving for this melty, cheesy dish. Cauliflower to the rescue yet again! This creamy sauce is absolutely packed with flavor and the addition of bacon makes this a standout dish. It's hearty enough to be served as a main dish or as a side dish for some flavorful grilled chicken.

Serves 8 ←

1 head of cauliflower, chopped into ½-inch (1-cm) squares
6 slices of bacon, chopped
1 cup (240 ml) heavy cream
2 oz (57 g) cream cheese
1 tbsp (15 ml) Worcestershire sauce
½ tsp ground mustard powder
¼ tsp onion powder
¼ tsp garlic powder
¼ tsp salt, plus more to serve
½ tsp xanthan gum
2 cups (226 g) sharp Cheddar cheese, divided
Ground pepper

Place the cauliflower in a microwave-safe bowl with 1 tablespoon (15 ml) of water. Cover the bowl with microwave-safe plastic wrap and microwave for 5 minutes. Drain well. Place the cauliflower in a medium baking dish.

In a medium saucepan, sauté the bacon over medium-high heat until crisped up. Remove the bacon from the pan and reserve the fat for another use, such as in the Bacon Blistered Green Beans (page 47).

In the same saucepan, combine the cream, cream cheese, Worcestershire sauce, mustard powder, onion powder, garlic powder and salt. Heat the mixture over medium-low heat. Stir to mix and warm.

Turn off the heat and whisk in the xanthan gum until it is well incorporated. Add 1½ cups (170 g) of Cheddar cheese and stir until melted. Add the bacon pieces into the cheese sauce and stir.

Pour the cheese mixture into a baking dish and mix with the cooked cauliflower. Cover the baking dish with foil and bake for 30 minutes. Uncover, add the remaining cheese and bake for 15 minutes uncovered. Season to taste with salt and pepper.

burrito shop cilantro-lime "rice"

This recipe is a delicious side to any spicy main. Toasting the riced cauliflower in coconut oil gives a rich roasted flavor, and the savory, spiced broth it's tossed with toward the end of cooking yields a delicious, flavorful dish. This cilantro-lime cauliflower rice beats the restaurant version in both cost and carb count.

Serves 4 ⬅

1 medium to large head of cauliflower
2 tbsp (27 g) refined coconut oil
2 tbsp (30 ml) lime juice
¼ cup (60 ml) chicken stock or broth
¼ tsp ground cumin
¼ tsp salt
¼ cup (4 g) chopped fresh cilantro

Cut the cauliflower florets from the stalk. Reserve the cauliflower stalk for use in another dish. Place the cauliflower florets in a food processor and pulse until it reaches rice-sized pieces.

Scrape the cauliflower rice into a microwave-safe bowl and add 2 tablespoons (30 ml) of water. Cover the bowl and microwave for 3 minutes. Drain the cauliflower rice in a stack of paper towels, kitchen towel or cheesecloth. Allow it to cool and then squeeze as much water as you can out of the rice.

Heat a nonstick pan over medium heat with the coconut oil. Place the cauliflower rice in the pan and sauté for 3 to 5 minutes in the oil until slightly golden brown. Add the lime juice, stock, cumin and salt. Turn the heat down to the lowest setting and continue to stir until the liquid has been absorbed into the toasted cauliflower rice.

Toss the mixture together with the cilantro and place it in a serving bowl. Best served warm!

sesame "fried" goat cheese balls

Sometimes simple really is best. Some dishes benefit from a variety of ingredients and flavors, others are magic by simply letting the main ingredients shine. I absolutely adore crispy fried goat cheese balls on a salad. This recipe has only two ingredients and is as simple as simple gets. Goat cheese has a lovely taste and texture when melted, and rolling them in sesame seeds before baking adds just the right amount of crunch. You don't need to batter and fry goat cheese in order to get those little balls of cheesy, crunchy deliciousness. The sesame seeds have just enough oil in them to crisp up in the oven during baking. They just don't need anything else! Serve with a simple oil and vinegar dressed salad.

Serves 6 to 8 ←

8 oz (226 g) goat cheese
¼ cup (36 g) sesame seeds
Leafy green salad with lemon juice or oil-and-vinegar dressing

Preheat the oven to 350°F (177°C, or gas mark 4). Line a baking sheet with parchment paper.

Portion the goat cheese into sixteen ½-ounce (14-g) servings. Roll into balls and then flatten slightly to form medallions. Coat each goat cheese medallion in the sesame seeds and place them on the baking sheet.

Bake for 10 minutes. Allow the cheese balls to cool before removing them from the baking sheet. Serve warm on a simple salad.

avocado tuna boats

Avocados are delicious and flavorful and creamy and expensive! I hate when I check an avocado only to find that it has passed its prime. While some people toss an avocado immediately after peak use, I have a hard time doing so. There are some cases when an avocado may be a bit mushy and will not stand up well to chopping for a salad but is still delicious and totally safe to eat! I use those avocados in this easy dish. All of the other ingredients are always on hand, and this comes together in less than 15 minutes.

Serves 4 ⬅

2 avocados, just past their prime
1 (4-oz [113-g]) can of tuna (any type), well-drained
2 tbsp (30 ml) mayo
1 tbsp (15 ml) lemon juice
Chopped celery (optional)
¼ cup (40 g) chopped red onion, divided
Salt and ground pepper

Cut each avocado in half and scoop out the flesh into a medium mixing bowl. Preserve the avocado skins to serve in.

Add the tuna to the avocado. Add the mayo, lemon juice and celery (if using). Stir to combine. Add three-quarters of the onion. Season to taste with salt and pepper.

Scoop the tuna-avocado filling into the avocado skins, sprinkle with the remaining onion and serve immediately.

bacon fried brussels sprouts

I never enjoyed Brussels sprouts until I had them roasted and crispy! I had always thought they were slimy and mushy and downright unappealing. After going low carb I began ordering crispy Brussels sprouts when available as a side in restaurants in place of a starchy vegetable. How are they so much more enjoyable in a restaurant? Well, because a lot of the time they are deep-fried to get that delicious crunch. I set out a way to make these at home without having to drag out the messy deep fryer. These are a wonderful starter or a side to a Ketogenic meal.

Serves 6 ←

1 lb (454 g) fresh Brussels sprouts
2 tbsp (28 g) bacon fat, melted
1 tbsp (30 ml) olive oil
½ tsp salt
1–2 tbsp (6–12 g) grated Parmesan cheese
Squeeze of fresh lemon juice

Preheat the oven to 375°F (190°C, or gas mark 5) and place a rack in the middle. Line a baking sheet with parchment paper.

Trim the stems off of each sprout and slice the sprouts in half. Save any leaves that fall off; these will make delicious crispy chips. Wash and drain the Brussels sprouts. Place them in a medium mixing bowl and drizzle in the bacon fat and olive oil. Toss to coat. Sprinkle with salt.

Spread the sprouts on the baking sheet. Turn the sprouts so that they are cut side down on the sheet. Bake for 30 minutes. Remove the baking sheet and turn the Brussels sprouts with a spatula. You just want to make sure that they have been tossed; they do not all need to be individually turned. Place them back in the oven for 10 to 15 minutes. Remove them when they are crispy and cooked through.

Place the Brussels sprouts in a serving dish. Sprinkle with Parmesan cheese and fresh lemon juice.

cheesy baked zucchini fritters

I absolutely love almost every variety of zucchini, and when it is in season it is one of the most affordable vegetables I can find. Sautéed in butter and olive oil with a sprinkle of salt is my go-to preparation. When I get sick of the simple sautéed version and have a fridge full of squash, I make a batch of these delicious zucchini fritters. The mixture can be prepared in advance and stored in the fridge until ready to bake up. They can also be fried!

Serves 4 ⬅

3 zucchini squash
1 egg
1 oz (28 g) cream cheese
¾ cup (78 g) almond flour
½ cup (50 g) ground walnuts, divided
¼ tsp onion powder
¼ tsp garlic powder
¼ cup (25 g) grated Parmesan cheese
½ tsp salt
Cheaper Than Bottled Ranch (page 126) or your favorite dipping sauce

Preheat the oven to 350°F (177°C, or gas mark 4). Line a baking sheet with parchment paper.

Grate the zucchini squash on a cheese grater. Place it in a microwave-safe bowl with ¼ cup (60 ml) of water and cover. Microwave for 5 minutes. Remove and allow it to cool. Pile the zucchini in a stack of paper towels or a kitchen towel and squeeze out as much water as possible.

Place the strained zucchini back in the bowl and add the egg, cream cheese, almond flour, ¼ cup (25 g) ground walnuts, onion powder, garlic powder, Parmesan and salt. Mix well.

Scoop out ¼-cup (60-g) servings and roll them in the remaining ground nuts. Place the fritters on the baking sheet. Bake for 12 to 15 minutes. Serve with ranch or your favorite dipping sauce.

caulimash

Cauliflower really can do it all. This recipe for mashed cauliflower is a great alternative to mashed potatoes. With the addition of a few simple spices, you'll have a delicious low-carb side that's sure to please everyone. Because cauliflower takes up flavors so well, storing this mashed cauliflower with some fresh sage (reserved from the roast recipe, page 13) imparts the loveliest flavor. This dish is wonderful prepared fresh or prepared ahead of time. I enjoy this side served with a pat of butter alongside One-Pan Roast Pork Tenderloin (page 17) or The Four-Hour Roast (page 13).

Serves 4 ←

1 head of cauliflower, chopped
¼ cup (60 ml) sour cream
2 tbsp (28 g) butter, melted, plus more for serving
¼ tsp garlic powder
¼ tsp salt
¼ tsp ground pepper
Fresh sage (optional)

Place the cauliflower in a microwave-safe bowl. Add 2 tablespoons (30 ml) of water and microwave, covered, for 8 to 10 minutes until tender. Drain the cauliflower and rinse with cool water.

Place the cauliflower on a stack of paper towels, kitchen towel or cheesecloth and squeeze out as much water as possible. Place the drained cauliflower in a food processor or blender and add the sour cream, butter, garlic powder, salt, pepper and sage (if using). Blend until smooth. Serve warm topped with a pat of butter.

spicy garlic buffalo wings

Dining out can get expensive, especially on a Ketogenic diet. While wings are naturally pretty Keto-friendly, running out for them all the time can become pretty costly. This spicy, garlic-flavored buffalo sauce is perfect for coating crispy wings baked at home. Skip the breading and you cut even more carbs. By baking wings that have been brushed with butter we get a super crispy wing that saves on dollars, carbs and cleanup!

Serves 4 to 6 ⬅

2 lb (907 g) chicken wings
¼ cup (57 g) butter, melted and divided
1 cup (240 ml) hot sauce, such as Frank's RedHot
1 tsp garlic powder
½ tsp cayenne pepper (optional)
¼ tsp xanthan gum
Blue cheese
Celery sticks

Preheat the oven to 375°F (190°C, or gas mark 5). If your oven has a convection setting, set it to 350°F (177°C) on convection. Line a baking sheet with parchment paper or place a baking rack on a baking sheet.

Pat the chicken wings dry and place them in a large mixing bowl. Pour 2 tablespoons (30 ml) of melted butter over the wings and toss them to make sure they are well coated. Spread them on the baking sheet. Bake for 45 minutes.

While the wings are baking, pour the remaining butter into a medium saucepan. Add the hot sauce along with the garlic powder and cayenne pepper (if using). Heat over medium-low for 3 to 5 minutes until smooth and well incorporated. Turn off the heat and whisk in the xanthan gum. The sauce will continue to thicken as it cools.

Remove the hot wings from the oven and allow them to cool for 5 minutes before coating them in half of the sauce. Reserve the other half of the sauce for dipping. Serve with blue cheese and celery.

cauliflower gratin

This rich, layered side dish is a great swap for the carb-heavy potatoes au gratin. It's thick and creamy and satisfying. Thinly sliced cauliflower is a perfect stand-in for the potato, and the onion and cheese in this recipe make it a proven winner.

Serves 6 ⬅

Butter

1 head of cauliflower

1 yellow onion, thinly sliced

1 cup (112 g) shredded sharp white Cheddar cheese

¼ tsp garlic powder

¼ tsp salt

Ground pepper

1 cup (240 ml) heavy whipping cream

Preheat the oven to 350°F (177°C, or gas mark 4). Grease a large casserole pan with butter.

Carefully remove all of the florets from the cauliflower and thinly slice them. Save all of the little pieces that may fall away during slicing. Trim the rough end off of the stem and preserve the stem for another dish.

Layer the bottom of the buttered baking dish with some cauliflower. Top that with one layer of onion. Add ⅓ cup (37 g) of Cheddar cheese. Repeat the process until all of the cauliflower, onion and cheese are spread in the dish. Whisk the garlic powder, salt and pepper into the heavy cream. Add the heavy cream slowly to the baking dish, being careful not to disturb the top cheese layer.

Cover it with foil and bake for 30 minutes. Uncover and bake for another 10 to 15 minutes until the top is golden brown. Allow the gratin to cool for 10 to 15 minutes before serving.

super frugal soups and salads

This chapter is all about Keto soups and salads. It's hard to find a Keto-friendly canned soup in the grocery store. Even soups with seemingly low-carb names are commonly packed with not-so-Keto-friendly additives, preservatives and sugars.

Salad dressings are in much the same boat. I've never found a shelf-stable creamy salad dressing that didn't contain some form of sugar in it! The salad dressing recipes in this chapter contain none of those ingredients. You can even measure out the dry ingredients in small jars and store them in your pantry. Never buy the sugar-packed packets of salad dressing seasoning again. It only takes a few minutes to add the wet ingredients and you will have a bottle of fresh ranch that beats the packets in price and carbs!

This chapter is full of delicious, convenient recipes that will keep your grocery bill and your carb count low!

"not so french" onion soup

Bubbly, melty cheese. I have always had a great love for cheese in all of its forms. In fact, I think that I used to order French onion soup as a child simply so that I could eat the cheese layer off of the top. While the base of this soup is pretty Keto-friendly on its own, the cheese floating above layers of bread or croutons is not. This recipe uses a thin layer of the Keto-friendly hamburger buns (page 105) as a cheese flotation device and drastically cuts down on the amount of onions in a traditional recipe. Cooking the onions low and slow will give this soup a lovely, rich flavor while skipping most of the carbs. You can also make the soup ahead of time and store it in the fridge until you are ready to broil it up and serve; this will also concentrate the onion flavors. I still enjoy the broiled cheese layer, but now I also clean my bowl.

Serves 4

2 tbsp (28 g) salted butter

2 tbsp (30 ml) olive oil

2 sweet yellow onions, thinly sliced

½ tsp salt

1 clove garlic, chopped

1½ tsp (1 g) thyme

1 bay leaf

¼ tsp ground pepper

1 tbsp (12 g) sweetener

4 cups (960 ml) beef broth or stock

Low-carb bread or a thin slice of You Can Have Buns Again Hamburger Buns (page 105), for toasting

Soft, white melty cheese such as Gruyère, provolone or mozzarella. Gruyère is the traditional choice, but not the only choice.

Heat the butter and olive oil over medium heat in a large saucepan. Add the onions and salt. Sauté the onions for 5 minutes, then reduce the heat to medium-low and continue to stir occasionally until the onions have caramelized and reached a rich brown color. This may seem time-consuming, but it is well worth it in terms of return on flavor. Continue to stir occasionally; it may take up to 20 minutes to develop a rich color and flavor.

Add the garlic and stir for 2 to 3 minutes until the garlic has softened. Add the thyme, bay leaf, pepper, sweetener and broth. Bring the soup up to a low simmer and cover. Allow the soup to simmer for at least 30 minutes. Turn off the heat and remove the bay leaf.

Preheat the oven to high or broiler setting. Spoon the soup into 4 ovenproof crocks. Slice a hamburger bun into large, thin strips. The shape and size of the hamburger bun makes it a great accompaniment to this dish, but feel free to use any low-carb bread you have available.

Place the soup crocks on a baking sheet for easy transportation into the oven. Top each bowl of soup with a handful of cheese. Place the baking sheet under the broiler or on the top rack for about 5 minutes. Watch the soup closely. Remove it when the cheese has browned and bubbled up. Serve immediately.

firehouse chili

When the weather starts to turn in the fall, nothing appeals to me more than a warm, spicy soup. When I first adopted a Ketogenic diet, I was shocked how many hidden sugars lurked in my favorite ready-to-go seasoning packets. Chili seasoning packets were surprisingly loaded with hidden carbs. Luckily, chili is super simple to prepare, and this recipe uses spices you probably already have in your collection. When ground beef is a good deal at the grocery store, I load up my cart and prepare a batch of my spicy firehouse chili. This recipe freezes well, too! Just allow it to cool and store it in gallon ziplock bags until you are ready to enjoy it. Cut the cayenne pepper in half if you prefer less spice in your chili.

Serves 6

¼ cup (57 g) butter

½ of a yellow onion, chopped

1 clove garlic, chopped

2 lb (907 g) ground beef

1 (14.5-oz [411-g]) can crushed or diced tomatoes

1 cup (240 ml) beef broth or stock, plus more if needed

1 tsp garlic powder

½ tsp onion powder

3 tbsp (18 g) chili powder

1 tbsp (7 g) smoked paprika

1 tsp cayenne pepper (optional)

1 tsp salt

Shredded Cheddar cheese (optional)

Thinly sliced green onions (optional)

Jalapeño Cheddar "Corn-less" Bread (page 96)

In a large saucepan over medium heat, melt the butter and then add the onion. Sauté over medium heat for 5 minutes, stirring frequently. Add the garlic and stir for 1 minute. Add the ground beef. Brown the meat for 10 minutes, stirring frequently. Using a spatula or wooden spoon, break up any large chunks as you go. Lower the heat to the lowest setting, simmer, if available.

Add the tomatoes, broth, garlic powder, onion powder, chili powder, paprika, cayenne (if using) and salt. Cover the pot and let simmer for 2 hours, stirring frequently. The onion and tomatoes will soften and almost melt into the chili. If the chili begins to seem too thick after 1 hour of cooking, thin it with more broth. The chili will be thick and rich when done.

This chili can also be moved into a slow cooker after all ingredients have been added and cooked on the medium setting for 3 to 4 hours. It can also be cooked on low for 8 hours. Like other chili, this is even better the next day! Serve topped with Cheddar cheese and green onions (if using) with the "corn-less" bread alongside.

skip-the-can cream of mushroom soup

Fresh mushrooms simmered in butter is something I could enjoy every day of the week. I rarely eat mushrooms raw, so I've picked up the habit of slicing them up and sautéing them right after I get home from the grocery store. They keep well for up to a week. If I have a container of sautéed mushrooms in my fridge that I need to use up, I toss them in my cream of mushroom soup! This soup is also a great way to use up trimmed, washed stems. Adding chopped up stems to the soup will add extra flavor and body as well. Since the soup will be blended, and skips the thickener, adding stems is a helpful addition. This soup can be made in advance and frozen for up to 3 months for a great homemade dish any time of the year.

Serves 6 ⬅

8 oz (226 g) fresh mushrooms, sliced
2 tbsp (28 g) butter
2 tbsp (20 g) finely chopped yellow onion
1 clove garlic, finely chopped
½ tsp salt, plus more to taste
1 ½ cups (360 ml) chicken broth
1 cup (240 ml) heavy cream
Ground pepper
1 egg yolk (optional)

For Serving (optional)
Butter
Chopped fresh parsley
Bacon
Shredded sharp white Cheddar cheese

In a medium saucepan over medium heat, sauté the mushrooms in the butter for 5 to 10 minutes until softened and slightly browned. Add the onion and garlic and sauté for 5 minutes. Add the salt and then pour in the broth. Lower the heat to low and simmer, uncovered, for 10 to 15 minutes to let all the flavors meld.

Turn off the heat and blend the soup using either an immersion blender or by carefully blending the soup in small batches in the blender. If you choose the blender method (my preferred method) make sure you are never filling the blender more than one-third of capacity. To make blending even safer, you can make the soup ahead of time and blend it in batches once cooled.

Once the soup is blended, return it to the saucepan and stir in the heavy cream. Add salt and pepper to taste. I start small with the salt and add more at the end. If you'd like to thicken the soup, turn off the heat and add the egg yolk while stirring vigorously.

Simmer the soup for 5 minutes before serving. This soup is delicious topped with a pat of butter, parsley, bacon or sharp white Cheddar cheese.

slow-simmered chicken bone broth

Chicken broth is a staple ingredient in my home. It may not be an expensive item to purchase, but I rarely have to buy it now that I've learned how to make my own chicken broth from leftovers! I usually have a quart in my fridge and several quarts in my freezer.

Chicken stock is a wonderful way to thin out savory sauces, a base for most of my soups and enjoyable in a mug in the colder months. This recipe uses nothing other than what would have been tossed in the trash, making it one of the most economical recipes anywhere. When prepping other dishes, I save my onion ends and skins, carrot shavings, celery leaves, all of it! I keep them in a big ziplock to throw into my chicken broth which I make once a week.

Makes at least 2 quarts (1.9 L) ←

2 or 3 chicken carcasses
Onion trimmings and skins
Celery trimmings and leaves
1–2 bay leaves
1 clove garlic, crushed
1 tbsp (15 ml) apple cider vinegar (optional)
1 tsp salt
1 tsp ground pepper

Additions (optional)
Whole peppercorns
Dried thyme
Fresh parsley

After removing all of the meat from a chicken, throw the bones of 2 or 3 carcasses into a large stockpot. Add all of the vegetable trimmings, bay leaves, garlic, vinegar (if using), salt, pepper and any additions you prefer (if using).

Cover with water and simmer for at least 8 hours and up to 24 hours on the lowest heat setting, covered. This can also be made in a slow cooker, but you will have less room so may need to reduce the number of chicken carcasses. Strain out the carcasses and vegetables and store the bone broth in the fridge or freezer.

white chicken chili

A great alternative to traditional chicken noodle soup, this recipe for white chicken chili uses shredded chicken in place of noodles and some fun additional spices. I make a batch of this chili when I have cooked chicken breasts in the fridge that I need to use up. It's somewhere between a soup and a stew in terms of texture and thickness. The shredded chicken provides a lot of body to this soup, so no carb-heavy thickeners are necessary!

Serves 4 ⬅

4 cups (960 ml) chicken stock or broth

8 oz (226 g) shredded leftover chicken

1 (4.5-oz [127-g]) can chopped green chilis, drained

1 tsp ground cumin

½ tsp garlic powder

½ tsp onion powder

½ tsp salt, plus more to taste

Ground pepper

Garnishes (optional)
Shredded Cheddar cheese

Sliced green onions

Fresh cilantro

Place the stock in a large saucepan. Bring it to a boil and then reduce the heat to low. Add the chicken, chilis, cumin, garlic powder, onion powder and salt. Simmer for 30 minutes, stirring occasionally. Season to taste with salt and pepper.

Ladle the chili into bowls and garnish with Cheddar cheese, green onions and cilantro (if using).

roasted cauliflower soup

Cauliflower has a reputation for being a great stand-in for potato in a low-carb diet and for good reason! It's an extremely versatile veggie. Because it is used in so many dishes, I tend to have a head in my fridge at all times. I made this soup for the first time when I had leftover Tasty Roasted Cauliflower Steaks (page 49). In fact, this soup can be made with many, many forms of leftover cauliflower dishes. I enjoy this soup simply with a pat of butter, a bit of sharp white Cheddar cheese and a generous sprinkling of fresh cracked pepper. You can also top a bowl of this soup with green onions, bacon crumbles and sour cream for a loaded "baked potato" or potato skin soup. Any way you serve it, this is a hearty and satisfying recipe that is both low carb and frugal. It can be prepared in advance and frozen for up to 3 months.

Serves 6 ⬅

1 head of cauliflower or 4 cups (496 g) leftover roasted cauliflower

1 tbsp (15 ml) olive oil

½ tsp salt, plus more to taste

2 tbsp (28 g) butter

½ cup (80 g) chopped yellow onion

4 cups (960 ml) chicken broth or stock, divided

½ cup (120 ml) heavy cream

Ground pepper

Preheat the oven to 350°F (177°C, or gas mark 4). Line a baking sheet with parchment paper.

To prepare fresh cauliflower: Chop the cauliflower into chunks no larger than 1 inch (2.5 cm) thick. Coat it in the olive oil and spread it over the baking sheet. Sprinkle it with the salt, and bake it in the oven for 30 minutes. Flip the cauliflower chunks over and roast them for another 15 minutes.

Alternatively, if you have roasted cauliflower left from making Tasty Roasted Cauliflower Steaks (page 49), Caulimash (page 64) or Cauliflower Gratin (page 68), use it instead.

While the cauliflower is roasting, heat a large saucepan over medium-low heat. Melt the butter in the pan and toss in the onion. Sauté for 5 to 10 minutes until soft. If the onion begins to brown too quickly, reduce the heat to low. Add half of the broth and simmer it, covered, until the cauliflower is finished roasting.

Add the roasted cauliflower to the broth. Add additional broth until the cauliflower is just covered with liquid. Cover and simmer on low for 30 minutes to allow all the flavors to meld.

Turn off the heat and blend the soup using an immersion blender or blend small batches in a traditional blender. If using this method, make sure to fill the pitcher no more than one-third full. Return the blended soup back into the large saucepan. Add the heavy cream. Season to taste with salt and pepper.

sandwich shop broccoli cheese soup

Nothing is more comforting than a giant bowl full of hot, cheesy broccoli soup. Even if you skip the bread bowl, this soup can be deceptively high in carbohydrates! Many premade soups include sugars and flours for thickener. This recipe utilizes the entire stalk of broccoli. This adds great flavor and body to the soup. This soup will satisfy just like that comforting classic with a much, much lower carb count and a lower price. This is great served with a sprinkling of shredded Cheddar cheese and a warm low-carb roll.

Serves 6 ⬅

2 tbsp (28 g) butter
¼ cup (40 g) chopped yellow onion
4 cups (960 ml) chicken stock or broth
1 head of broccoli
1 tsp onion powder
½ tsp garlic powder
2 tbsp (29 g) cream cheese
2 cups (226 g) shredded Cheddar cheese, plus more for serving
½ cup (120 ml) heavy cream
½ tsp xanthan gum
½ tsp salt
Cooked chicken (optional)

Warm the butter in a large saucepan over medium heat. Add the onion. Sauté for 5 to 10 minutes until the onion is softened. Reduce the heat to low and add the stock.

Trim the stem of the broccoli head and then chop the entire head of broccoli into small chunks, about a ½- to 1-inch (1- to 2.5-cm) cubes. Add all of the stems to the saucepan. Sift through the pieces of broccoli chopped from the stems and save any small pieces, ½ inch (1 cm) or smaller. Set aside. Add the rest of the broccoli into the saucepan.

Add the onion powder, garlic powder and cream cheese. Cover and simmer for 20 to 30 minutes, until the broccoli has softened.

Blend the soup with an immersion blender or in small batches in a traditional blender. Once the soup is well blended, add the Cheddar cheese, heavy cream, xanthan gum and salt. Stir well over the lowest heat setting. Add in the smallest pieces of broccoli and continue to stir until the soup is smooth.

Add chicken for extra protein if you prefer, and top with more cheese right before serving!

the best cobb salad

Finding a Cobb salad in a restaurant is exciting. The toppings are a collection of super Keto-friendly ingredients, and it's usually served with a delicious low-carb blue cheese dressing. Once these salads became part of my eating-out life, I started craving them at home. The toppings, being Keto staples, are usually in my fridge at all times. All I needed to do was find the perfect blue cheese dressing. This dressing uses classic ingredients that are easy to find. Although blue cheese may sometimes be a spendy item, making this dressing yourself will save you money and offset the costs. This dressing will keep for up to a week in the fridge, and it also makes a great dip for veggies.

Serves 4 ⬅

Blue Cheese Dressing
½ cup (120 ml) sour cream
½ cup (120 ml) mayo
1 tsp vinegar
¼ tsp Worcestershire sauce
¼ tsp garlic powder
¼ tsp salt
¼ tsp ground pepper
½ cup (68 g) crumbled blue cheese

Salad
Chopped lettuce
Chopped chicken
Shredded cheese
Sliced avocado
Crumbled bacon
Chopped tomato
Hard-boiled egg, halved

To make the blue cheese dressing: Combine the sour cream and mayo in a medium-sized bowl. Add the vinegar, Worcestershire sauce, garlic powder, salt and pepper. Whisk all the ingredients together until smooth. Add the blue cheese crumbles and gently fold them in.

To make the salad: Assemble as many toppings as you prefer and top with blue cheese dressing.

Store leftover dressing in a glass jar in the fridge. It keeps for up to 2 weeks.

the real deal chicken caesar salad

The first time I had an authentic Caesar dressing I thought I had died and gone to heaven. It is a slightly time-consuming salad dressing to prepare, but the result is so worth a bit of elbow grease. This dressing is rich and delicious and tastes nothing like store-bought Caesar dressings. Salads may seem like a boring Keto staple, but this recipe is anything but ordinary. Tasty, extremely low carb and affordable, this dressing checks all the boxes.

Serves 4 ←

Salad
1 head of romaine lettuce
Leftover chicken, chopped

Dressing
1 egg yolk
2 tbsp (30 ml) lemon juice
2 cloves garlic, finely chopped
1 tsp anchovy paste
½ cup (120 ml) light olive oil
¼ cup (60 ml) extra virgin olive oil
¼ cup (25 g) grated Parmesan cheese, plus more for serving
¼ tsp salt
Ground black pepper
Lemon wedges

To prepare the salad: Rip up, wash and drain the head of romaine lettuce. Allow the lettuce to dry on a kitchen towel.

To make the dressing: In a medium mixing bowl, combine the egg yolk and lemon juice. Whisk until well combined. Stir in the garlic and the anchovy paste. Add both olive oils to a measuring cup with a pouring spout. Starting very slowly, drizzle the oil into the lemon and yolk while whisking. Whisk briskly and take occasional breaks from adding the oil but continue to whisk. Slowly drizzle the rest of the oil into the dressing while whisking. This should take at least 2 minutes. The dressing should be thickened, but not as firm as a mayonnaise. Add the Parmesan and fold it in. Add the salt and season to taste with pepper. I usually add an extra crank of fresh pepper.

To make the salad: Pour half of the Caesar dressing into a clean, dry mixing bowl. Add the romaine lettuce to the bowl and toss it in the dressing. Plate the salad and top it with chicken. Add a bit more Parmesan and cracked pepper to the chicken. Serve the remainder of the dressing on the side along with a lemon wedge for extra zip.

creamy keto egg salad

Having a stash of hard-boiled eggs in your fridge will never let you down, especially when starting a Ketogenic diet. They are a quick, frugal and super simple snack that is as Keto-friendly as they come. Sometimes you need to use up those eggs. This recipe will give you a tasty new dish that ensures your boiled egg stash will never go to waste.

Serves 2

6 hard-boiled eggs, peeled and chopped
¼ cup (60 ml) mayo
1 tbsp (15 ml) mustard
½ of an overripe avocado
1 tsp white wine or rice wine vinegar
½ cup (41 g) chopped cooked bacon
½ tsp celery seeds
½ tsp dried dill
¼ tsp salt
¼ tsp ground pepper

For Serving (optional)
Soft Ciabatta Rolls (page 101)
Bibb or Boston lettuce leaves

Place the chopped eggs in a large mixing bowl. In a medium mixing bowl, combine the mayo, mustard, avocado, vinegar, bacon, celery seeds, dill, salt and pepper. Whisk the dressing to combine. Spoon this mixture into the large mixing bowl with the chopped eggs. Fold the dressing into the chopped eggs.

I like to serve this on a roll, in a leaf of lettuce or simply on its own!

steak house wedge salad

A simple wedge salad is a beautiful and delicious option at many steak houses. The lettuce, dressing and toppings are commonly Keto-friendly, but the glazes are not. Balsamic dressing is a bit higher on the carb count than other vinegars and when thickened and sweetened in a glaze it's very high. This recipe uses a clever swap to incorporate the wonderful flavors of a balsamic glaze while skipping the carbs. Sugar-free or low-carb syrups are an amazing and versatile Keto staple. They're great for thickening sauces and adding flavor and sweetness. This recipe is a total crowd-pleaser, and it will delight even the non-low-carb dieters.

Serves 4

Balsamic Reduction

¼ cup (60 ml) balsamic vinegar

1 tbsp (15 ml) water

2 tbsp (30 ml) sugar-free breakfast syrup

Salad

1 head of Bibb or iceberg lettuce

1 cup (240 ml) blue cheese dressing (page 87)

1 cup (82 g) chopped cooked bacon

½ cup (68 g) crumbled blue cheese

A few cherry tomatoes, halved

Ground pepper

To make the glaze: In a small saucepan, bring the balsamic vinegar, water and sugar-free syrup to a simmer. Allow the mixture to simmer for 10 minutes until thickened. Allow it to cool.

To make the salad: Chop the head of lettuce in half and then chop those halves in half again. Rinse the 4 quarters of lettuce well and allow them to drain on a kitchen towel or paper towel. Place each lettuce wedge on a plate and top each with one-quarter of the blue cheese dressing, bacon and crumbled blue cheese. Top with cherry tomatoes and season with pepper. Drizzle the salad with the balsamic vinegar reduction just before serving.

beats the bake shop breads and rolls

By far the hardest thing to give up when adopting a Ketogenic diet is the bread. I think that I liked bread more than candy or desserts or any other food group in existence. Warm rolls right out of the oven smothered with butter are pretty hard to beat. This chapter is full of recipes that will satisfy that craving!

Here you'll find Pizza Shop Garlic Knots (page 95), Herbed Olive Oil Focaccia (page 98) and a basic hamburger bun recipe (page 105) that's perfect for the Chili-Lime Chicken Burgers (page 18) or Black and Blue Burgers (page 21). There are muffins and breads that will make a perfect accompaniment to afternoon tea or coffee. There is a way to Keto-fy almost every bread out there, and you'll find some tasty recipes in this chapter that do just that!

pizza shop garlic knots

There's nothing better than a foil wrapper full of hot, garlicky knots of pizza dough. Once I gave up traditional pizza shops, I also gave up those buttery delights. Not anymore! This recipe for Pizza Shop Garlic Knots will make a perfect accompaniment to Carb-Cutting Eggplant Parmesan (page 31), Scanty Shrimp Scampi (page 22) or Spicy Sausage with Collards (page 38). Add these fun little knots of dough to a dish and you'll feel like you haven't given anything up.

Serves 8

3 cups (336 g) shredded mozzarella
1 egg
1 cup (104 g) almond flour
1 tsp baking powder
½ tsp garlic powder
2 tbsp (30 ml) melted butter
Salt

Preheat the oven to 350°F (177°C, or gas mark 4). Line a baking sheet with parchment paper.

Place the mozzarella into a microwave-safe bowl and microwave for 1 minute. Stir the cheese to make sure that the edges aren't cooking against the side of the bowl. If there are any shreds of cheese that aren't melted, place the bowl back in the microwave for 15 seconds at a time until thoroughly melted. Add the egg to the cheese and stir until well combined.

In a separate bowl, combine the almond flour, baking powder and garlic powder. Whisk the dry ingredients together and then add them to the cheese mixture. Stir to combine.

Once the dough is well mixed, knead it for several minutes until the dough ball is firm and holds together well.

Roll the dough out into a large square. Cut the dough into 8 long strips. Take one strip and roll it out in front of you with the palm of your hand. Tie each strip of dough into a knot and place it on the baking sheet. Repeat with each strip. Bake for 10 to 12 minutes until golden brown. Brush with melted butter and sprinkle with salt.

jalapeño cheddar "corn-less" bread

While some dishes are super simple to convert into a Keto-friendly version, like my Firehouse Chili (page 75), they just don't feel quite complete without the carb-loaded sides we're used to enjoying with them. This low-carb "corn-less" bread is a perfect accompaniment to chili or served simply on its own! It's best served warm with a pat of butter.

Serves 12 ←

Oil or butter

4 eggs

1 oz (29 g) cream cheese

¼ cup (60 ml) sour cream

1 tbsp (12 g) sweetener, such as Lakanto or Truvia (optional)

2 cups (208 g) almond flour

1 tsp baking powder

½ tsp salt

¼ tsp garlic powder

½ cup (57 g) shredded Cheddar cheese

¼ cup (36 g) chopped jalapeños

Preheat the oven to 350°F (177°C, or gas mark 4) and place a rack in the middle. Oil or butter an 8 x 8–inch (20 x 20–cm) baking dish and set aside.

In a large mixing bowl, combine the eggs, cream cheese, sour cream and sweetener (if using). Mix well with a hand mixer.

In a separate bowl, stir together the almond flour, baking powder, salt and garlic powder. Once the dry ingredients are well combined, pour them into the bowl with the wet mixture. Stir or blend with a hand mixer on low until all of the ingredients are well incorporated.

Add the Cheddar cheese and the jalapeños and fold them into the mixture with a spoon or spatula. Pour the batter into the greased baking dish and bake for 30 to 40 minutes. Allow the bread to cool before slicing.

herbed olive oil focaccia

Focaccia is one of my absolute favorite breads. I love to serve it with a bowl of olive oil seasoned with salt and pepper for dipping. Just because you have given up the carbs does not mean you have to give up your favorite things! This recipe for herbed focaccia is an excellent accompaniment to any savory main, as a side for a salad or even sliced and used as a sandwich bread. Add some seasoned chicken with a lettuce leaf and some Caesar dressing for an outstanding lunch!

Serves 8 ⬅

3 cups (336 g) shredded mozzarella

2 tbsp (29 g) cream cheese

1 egg

1 cup (104 g) almond flour

1 tsp baking powder

¼ tsp onion powder

¼ tsp garlic powder

1 tsp dried rosemary

Olive oil

Salt and ground pepper

Preheat the oven to 350°F (177°C, or gas mark 4). Line a baking sheet with parchment paper.

Melt the mozzarella in a microwave-safe bowl for 30 seconds. Add the cream cheese. Stir the mozzarella and place the bowl back in the microwave for 30 seconds at a time until the cheese is completely melted. Add the egg to the cheese mixture and stir with a wooden spoon until incorporated.

In a separate bowl, whisk the almond flour, baking powder, onion powder, garlic powder and rosemary together. Add the dry ingredients to the cheese mixture and stir to combine. The dough may get firm and hard to stir with a spoon. If this happens you can wet your hands with water and knead the dough until smooth.

Spread the dough onto the baking sheet. Press it into a square about 10 x 10 inches (25 x 25 cm). Brush the top with some olive oil and sprinkle with salt and pepper.

Press your fingers into the surface of the dough to make tiny indentations over the whole surface. It's okay to press all the way through the dough to the baking sheet, the dough will spread back together while cooking. Bake for 20 to 25 minutes until golden brown. Enjoy dipped in olive oil seasoned with salt and ground pepper.

*See photo on page 92.

flexible tortilla wraps

These ultra-low-carb, flexible wraps are an excellent vehicle for soft tacos, fajitas (page 10) or even breakfast burritos. They are a bit more delicate than a traditional, carb-heavy tortilla but well worth the effort. These can be made ahead of time and stored, stacked, in a ziplock bag in the fridge.

Makes 8 ←

4 egg whites
½ tsp salt, divided
¼ cup (60 ml) almond milk, unsweetened
2 tbsp (14 g) coconut flour
1 tbsp (7 g) almond flour
1 tbsp (8 g) psyllium husks
1 tsp baking powder
¼ tsp xanthan gum

Preheat the oven to 350°F (177°C, or gas mark 4). Line a baking sheet with parchment paper.

In a medium mixing bowl, combine the egg whites and ¼ teaspoon salt. Whip the egg whites into stiff peaks. Add the almond milk and stir gently.

In a separate bowl, add the coconut flour, almond flour, psyllium husks, baking powder, the remaining salt and xanthan gum. Whisk the dry mixture to combine and then add it to the egg whites. Gently fold all the ingredients together until well incorporated.

These flexible tortillas can be baked or fried in a skillet. Because they are very delicate until cooled, I prefer to bake them. Place ¼ cup (60 ml) of the tortilla batter on the baking sheet. Spread the batter out into a 4-inch (10-cm) circle. You will be able to fit 4 tortillas on a baking sheet at once. Bake for 8 to 10 minutes. Allow the tortillas to cool completely before removing them from the baking sheet.

If you prefer frying, heat a nonstick skillet over medium-low heat. Pour in ¼ cup (60 ml) of batter and swirl the pan to coat the bottom with batter. Cook for 3 to 5 minutes, then flip and cook the other side for 2 to 3 minutes.

Stack the tortillas with a piece of parchment paper between each one until you're ready to use them. These go great with At-Home Fajitas (page 10).

*See photo on page 11.

soft ciabatta rolls

These rolls are chewy and delicious. I love using them for sandwiches or enjoyed alone with a pat of butter right out of the oven. They are an excellent choice for a packed lunch.

Makes 4 👈

2 cups (224 g) shredded mozzarella cheese
1 egg
1 cup (104 g) almond flour
½ cup (50 g) grated Parmesan cheese
1 tsp baking powder
¼ tsp onion powder

Preheat the oven to 350°F (177°C, or gas mark 4) and place a rack in the middle. Line a baking sheet with parchment paper.

Place the mozzarella cheese in a microwave-safe bowl. Microwave for 30 seconds and then stir the cheese. Microwave for 30 seconds. Stir. Continue to repeat short bursts in the microwave until the cheese is completely melted. Crack an egg in the bowl and stir the egg and the cheese together with a wooden spoon.

In a separate bowl, combine the almond flour, Parmesan cheese, baking powder and onion powder. Mix well. Add the dry mixture to the cheese and egg. Stir to combine. Once you have mixed as well as you can with a wooden spoon, knead with your hands until the dough is completely uniform. You may still see small chunks of Parmesan in the dough, this is fine!

Divide the dough into 4 equal sections and roll each section into a ball. Place them on the baking sheet and bake for 15 to 20 minutes until golden brown. Allow the rolls to cool fully before removing them from the baking sheet.

snickerdoodle muffins

Snickerdoodle cookies have always been a favorite. I love the way the coating gives the cookies an almost crispy surface. These muffins have the same sweet cinnamon punch on the surface with a rich, moist and cakey vanilla center—but without the carbs! I love these as a snack or with a cup of cinnamon-spiced tea.

Makes 12 ⬅

3 eggs
3 tbsp (42 g) softened butter
¼ cup (58 g) cream cheese
¼ cup (60 ml) sour cream
1 tsp vanilla extract
½ cup (96 g) sweetener
1 tsp cinnamon
1¾ cups (182 g) almond flour
2 tsp (9 g) baking powder

Topping
¼ tsp cinnamon
1 tbsp (12 g) granulated sweetener

Preheat the oven to 350°F (177°C, or gas mark 4). Line a 12-well muffin pan.

To make the muffins: In a large bowl combine the eggs, butter, cream cheese, sour cream, vanilla and sweetener. Blend with a hand mixer on the lowest setting.

In a separate bowl, combine the cinnamon, almond flour and baking powder. Stir the dry ingredients together and then add them to the wet mixture in the large bowl. Fold the wet and dry ingredients together. Spoon ¼ cup (60 ml) of the muffin batter into each well of the muffin pan.

To make the topping: In a small bowl, mix the cinnamon with the sweetener.

Sprinkle the topping evenly over the 12 muffins. Bake for 25 to 30 minutes. Allow the muffins to cool for at least 10 minutes before serving.

you can have buns again hamburger buns

My best advice to anyone starting a Ketogenic diet is to begin by simply skipping the bun. Ordering a burger without the bun is a great start. After a while though, I certainly began to miss buns. This recipe will yield a delicious, toastable burger bun. Maybe it's the feeling of biting into the bread, or simply the act of holding a burger again, but these buns make me feel like I'm missing nothing! Making your own bread substitutions is a delicious and frugal way to make sure that you don't miss the bun either.

Serves 4 ←

3 cups (336 g) shredded mozzarella cheese
1 egg
1½ cups (156 g) almond flour
1 tsp baking powder

Preheat the oven to 350°F (177°C, or gas mark 4) and place a rack in the middle. Line a baking sheet with parchment paper.

Add the mozzarella cheese to a microwave-safe bowl. Microwave for 30 seconds and then stir the cheese. Microwave for 30 seconds. Stir. Continue to repeat short bursts in the microwave until the cheese is completely melted. Crack the egg into the bowl and stir the egg and the cheese together with a wooden spoon.

In a separate bowl, combine the almond flour and baking powder. Mix well. Add the dry mixture to the cheese mixture. Stir to combine. Once you have mixed as well as you can with a wooden spoon, knead with your hands until the dough is completely uniform.

Divide the dough into 4 equal sections and roll each section into a ball. Place the buns on the baking sheet and bake for 15 to 20 minutes until golden brown. Allow the buns to cool fully before removing them from the baking sheet.

budget-friendly breakfast and brunch

The Ketogenic diet has been called the bacon and eggs diet. And that's true! Bacon and eggs are extremely Keto-friendly choices. But there are so many more options for breakfast and brunch than just the basics! This chapter is full of creative dishes that will help you expand your breakfast and brunch options. From delicious fluffy pancakes (page 108) to blintzes (page 111) to quiche (page 112), this chapter has you covered. Feel like putting out a fancy spread on a Sunday? I've even included a Keto-friendly recipe for a pastry platter (page 115) that will satisfy any sweet tooth. A low-carb brunch does not need to be boring. This chapter provides recipes that are sure to please.

better than the diner pancakes

I love pancakes, but after going low carb I searched high and low for a great Keto pancake recipe and was always disappointed. Every single one missed the mark. The first time I made this recipe I may have cried. Okay, I cried. They smell like pancakes. They look like pancakes and, most importantly, they taste like real pancakes! After they come off the griddle, brush each one with a bit of melted butter mixed with your favorite low-carb syrup. Trust me, you won't be disappointed.

Makes 8 pancakes ⬅

2 oz (57 g) cream cheese
2 eggs
2 tbsp (30 ml) melted butter
Dash of vanilla extract
2 oz (57 g) almond flour (about ½ cup)
2 tsp (9 g) baking powder
1 tbsp (7 g) coconut flour
2 tbsp (24 g) sweetener, such as Truvia or Lakanto
4 egg whites, whipped (optional)
Butter
Sugar-free breakfast syrup

Combine the cream cheese, eggs, butter and vanilla together until well blended; you can use a hand mixer or a blender to combine. In a medium bowl, stir the almond flour, baking powder, coconut flour and sweetener together. Add the dry ingredients into the wet and stir to combine. The mixture will be thick.

For lighter, fluffier pancakes, fold in the optional egg whites.

These pancakes need to be cooked a bit lower and slower than traditional pancakes. Butter a nonstick skillet and heat over medium-low. Pour ⅓ cup (80 ml) of batter in the center of the skillet and cook for 3 to 5 minutes per side. The batter will spread out as it warms in the skillet. You will get bubbles on the surface when they are ready to be flipped—just like a traditional pancake.

This batter can be prepared ahead of time and kept in the fridge. These can also be cooked, stacked between pieces of parchment paper in a ziplock bag and then frozen for a super quick breakfast. When retrieving them from the freezer, the paper makes for easy removal! Just remove the pancakes from the bag and microwave for 45 seconds. Top with butter and sugar-free breakfast syrup!

easter brunch blintzes

There's nothing I enjoy more than a beautiful brunch buffet. Rows and rows of lovely breakfast foods, some classics and some standouts. A food that I always found on the buffet that I never made at home was the blintz. Rich and creamy and covered in a fruit syrup and whipped cream. I skip the buffet version now, but I make my own Keto-friendly filled blintz at home. Sweetened, whipped ricotta cheese takes the place of the sugary filling and whipped cream. Enjoy these with some sugar-free raspberry jam (page 116).

Serves 4 ←

Crepes
8 eggs
8 oz (226 g) cream cheese
¼ cup (48 g) sweetener
½ tsp vanilla extract
1 tbsp (7 g) almond flour
Butter or coconut oil
Sugar-free syrup

Filling
8 oz (226 g) full-fat ricotta cheese
¼ cup (30 g) powdered sweetener
½ tsp vanilla extract

To make the crepes: Blend the eggs, cream cheese, sweetener, vanilla and almond flour together in a blender. In a medium-sized, nonstick skillet, melt about a teaspoon of butter over medium-low heat. Pour ⅓ cup (80 ml) of crepe batter into the skillet and cook for 3 to 5 minutes per side. These crepes are extremely delicate. Take care when flipping. I usually use two spatulas to flip them. When the crepe has finished cooking, stack it on a plate. Melt another teaspoon of butter to the pan and repeat the process until you have used up all the batter. The recipe will make 8 crepes.

To make the filling: In a medium mixing bowl, combine the ricotta cheese, powdered sweetener and vanilla. Whip up the mixture with a hand mixer until smooth and fluffy, about 3 minutes.

Fill each crepe with one-eighth of the filling mixture and fold over. Serve warm with sugar-free syrup.

onion bacon quiche

This delicious quiche can be prepared with or without a crust. For those looking for the classic quiche experience, I've included an extremely Keto-friendly crust recipe. The rich, buttery crust can be prepared in advance and cooked up with the filling right before serving. This is an easy brunch dish that won't break the bank.

Serves 6 ⬅

Crust
1 cup (104 g) almond flour
½ tsp salt
2 tbsp (28 g) salted butter

Filling
6–8 slices of bacon, chopped
¼ cup (40 g) chopped yellow onion
4 eggs
1 cup (240 ml) heavy cream
¼ tsp salt
1 cup (113 g) shredded white Cheddar cheese

Preheat the oven to 350°F (177°C, or gas mark 4) and place a rack at the bottom.

To make the crust: In a medium mixing bowl, combine the almond flour, salt and butter. Cut into the mixture with a pastry cutter until well incorporated. The crust doesn't need to be completely uniform in texture, just mixed enough so that the chunks of butter are about the size of a pea. Spread the mixture in the bottom of a tart pan or 8- to 10-inch (20- to 25-cm) pie pan. Press the mixture into the bottom of the pan until it is firm. The layer should be even. Bake the crust for 10 minutes. Remove the crust from the oven and prepare the filling.

To make the filling: In a medium-sized skillet over medium heat, cook the bacon until crisped, 5 to 10 minutes. Reserve 1 tablespoon (15 ml) of bacon fat and sauté the onion over medium heat for 5 minutes until the onion is translucent and softened. Drain. In a medium mixing bowl, combine the eggs and cream. Whip them together. Fold the salt and cheese into the egg mixture. Add the bacon and onion to the mixture.

To make the quiche: Pour the filling over the prebaked crust. Bake the quiche for 25 to 30 minutes until set. Allow it to cool for at least 10 minutes before serving.

keto pastry platter

A brunch favorite of mine has always been a beautiful array of pastries. Traditional pastries are something I have learned to skip, but not at home! These mini Keto pastries are both lovely and delicious. The tiny dough squares are filled with a sweetened cream cheese mixture and topped with a variety of nuts. It's a beautiful, tasty and frugal addition to any Keto brunch.

Makes 12 small pastries ←

Filling

4 oz (113 g) cream cheese
2 tbsp (24 g) sweetener
¼ tsp vanilla extract
1 tbsp (15 ml) heavy cream

Dough

2½ cups (280 g) shredded mozzarella cheese
1 cup (104 g) almond flour
¼ cup (30 g) powdered sweetener
½ tsp baking powder

For Topping (optional)

1 egg
Nuts of your choice, such as sliced almonds

Preheat the oven to 350°F (177°C, or gas mark 4). Line a baking sheet with parchment paper.

To make the filling: Whip up the cream cheese, sweetener, vanilla and heavy cream in a medium bowl. Set aside.

To make the dough: In a medium, microwave-safe bowl, melt the mozzarella cheese in 30-second increments, stirring at each increment, until smooth. Add the almond flour, sweetener and baking powder. Knead until smooth. Roll the dough out and cut it into 12 squares.

To make the pastry: Place a dollop of filling in the center of each square and fold over. Brush the surface of the pastry with an egg wash (if using) for a beautiful sheen. Top with optional nuts of your choice. Bake on the baking sheet for 8 to 10 minutes until golden brown. Allow the pastry to cool for 3 to 5 minutes before arranging on a platter.

classic scones with raspberry jam

A classic, crumbly, barely sweet scone is completely possible on a low-carb diet, and this jam is the perfect accompaniment. Raspberries are one of the lowest carb fruits out there, and if you freeze them in half-pound (226-g) bags when they are in season, you'll be able to enjoy this jam all year round for pennies per serving.

Makes 6 scones ⬅

Scones
¼ cup (57 g) butter
2 eggs
¼ cup (48 g) sweetener
1 tsp vanilla extract
2 tbsp (30 ml) heavy cream
1 tsp baking powder
2 cups (208 g) almond flour
¼ cup (28 g) coconut flour

Jam
1 (8–12-oz [226–340-g]) bag of frozen raspberries
½ cup (120 ml) water
¼ cup (48 g) sweetener
1 tbsp (15 ml) lemon juice
½ tsp xanthan gum
2 tbsp (20 g) chia seeds

Preheat the oven to 350°F (177°C, or gas mark 4). Line a baking sheet with parchment paper.

To make the scones: Melt the butter in a medium, microwave-safe bowl. Add the eggs, sweetener and vanilla and whisk until the mixture is smooth. Add the heavy cream and stir.

In a large mixing bowl, add the baking powder, almond flour and coconut flour. Stir to combine. Pour the wet mixture into the bowl with the dry mixture. Draw the blade of a butter knife through the mixture while rotating the bowl. Do not overmix. Keep dragging the knife through the mixture while rotating the bowl until you have a crumbly mix and no crumbles larger than a pea are present.

Pile the dough in the center of the baking sheet and form it into a circle. Gently press the dough down and keep scooting the dough in from the sides to create a 7- to 8-inch (18- to 20-cm) circle. Cut through the center of the dough circle but leave the dough intact; don't pull the sides away from each other. Cut the dough at an angle, all the way through, about a third of the circle. Cut the remaining section in two to create 6 equal pieces.

Bake for 15 to 18 minutes until golden brown. Allow the scones to cool completely before removing them from the baking sheet.

While the scones bake, make the jam. Bring the raspberries, water, sweetener and lemon juice to a boil in a small saucepan. Lower the heat and simmer for 10 minutes. Remove the saucepan from the heat. Whisk in the xanthan gum and chia seeds. The mixture will thicken as it cools.

Once your scones and jam have cooled, transfer the scones to a platter with the jam served on the side. Store any leftover jam in a glass jar in the fridge for up to 1 week.

french toast-less toast

Enjoy this recipe for "toastless" French toast any time of day. This dish cooks up in a large baking dish and then is sliced into little triangle-shaped servings. To heat up and enjoy, simply warm the slices in a small skillet with some butter! These slices are fantastic for a weekend brunch spread, and they're wonderful topped with sweetened whipped cream and some powdered Keto-friendly sweetener or sugar-free syrup. This dish can be prepared in advance and stored in the fridge.

Serves 4 ←

8 oz (226 g) cream cheese
8 eggs
¼ cup (48 g) sweetener
2 tbsp (13 g) almond flour
1 tsp baking powder
1 tsp vanilla extract
Sugar-free breakfast syrup, for serving

Preheat the oven to 350°F (177°C, or gas mark 4). Line a lasagna pan with parchment paper.

Combine the cream cheese, eggs, sweetener, almond flour, baking powder and vanilla in a blender. Starting on low, blend the mixture until completely incorporated.

Pour the batter into the lasagna pan and bake for 30 minutes. Slice into 4 large squares. Slice those squares diagonally to make 8 triangle portions.

You can serve the French toast immediately or store it in a ziplock bag in the fridge. Toast it up in butter in a skillet when you are ready to enjoy. Serve it topped with the sugar-free breakfast syrup.

dollar-saving dips, chips and sauces

Party food! You really don't have to give up anything when adopting a Ketogenic lifestyle. You definitely do not need to give up chips and dips! There are a few clever swaps we'll use in this chapter to make sure that crunch is something that won't be missing from your Ketogenic diet. From the Crispy Parmesan Chips (page 122) to Guacamole with Pepperoni Chips (page 134), you'll be able to enjoy anything that you used to dip traditional chips into. The Bacon Jalapeño Popper Dip (page 125) will be sure to please even your carb-loving friends. This chapter is loaded with recipes that are tasty, low carb and wallet-friendly.

crispy parmesan chips

If you're missing crunch on a Ketogenic diet, I have you covered. Store-bought cheese chips can be hard to find and very expensive. It is so easy to make these chips yourself! This recipe ensures you'll never have to buy Parmesan chips again.

Makes 24 chips ⬅

1 (8-oz [226-g]) container of shredded, grated or shaved Parmesan cheese (make sure the container says 100% Parmesan)
Bacon Jalapeño Popper Dip (page 125) or Does-It-All Spinach Dip (page 133)

Preheat the oven to 375°F (190°C, or gas mark 5). If the oven has a convection setting, set it to 350°F (177°C) on convection. Place a rack in the middle of the oven. Line a mini muffin pan with liners.

Pulse the Parmesan cheese in a food processor a few times; smaller pieces make measuring it easier. Place 1 tablespoon (8 g) of Parmesan cheese in each well of the lined muffin pan. Bake for 8 minutes.

Remove the muffin pan from the oven and pop the cheese crisps out of the liners onto a cooling rack. Reuse muffin liners until you have baked the desired amount of crispy Parmesan crisps. Serve the crisps with dip.

fantastic homemade blue cheese dressing

I so enjoy the rich flavorful addition of blue cheese to almost anything. Blue cheese dressing is wonderful on a salad or as a dip for fresh vegetables. Store-bought, shelf-stable blue cheese dressing tends to be higher in sugar than it needs to be. This recipe is quick and simple and easy on the wallet.

Serves 6

½ cup (120 ml) sour cream
½ cup (120 ml) mayo
1 tsp white, white wine or rice wine vinegar
¼ tsp Worcestershire sauce
¼ tsp salt, plus more to taste
¼ tsp ground pepper, plus more to taste
¼ tsp garlic powder
½ cup (68 g) crumbled blue cheese

In a medium mixing bowl, combine the sour cream, mayo, vinegar and Worcestershire sauce. Whisk it together until smooth. Add the salt, pepper and garlic powder. Continue to whisk the dressing until the seasonings are well incorporated. Add the blue cheese to the dressing and fold in with a spatula or wooden spoon.

Season the dressing to taste with salt and pepper. Store any unused portion in the refrigerator; it will keep for up to 1 week.

*See photo on page 86.

bacon jalapeño popper dip

There's something about the combination of smoky bacon and jalapeños that really hits the spot. This dip will satisfy the popper craving without all of the carbs you would get with the breading. You can use canned jalapeños in this recipe or even substitute green chilis for great flavor with a bit less spice.

Serves 8 ←

8 oz (226 g) cream cheese

½ cup (120 ml) sour cream

½ cup (120 ml) ranch dressing

¼ tsp garlic powder

¼ tsp onion powder

¼ tsp salt

1 cup (113 g) shredded Cheddar cheese

¼ cup (36 g) chopped jalapeños or green chiles

6 slices of bacon, cooked, cooled and chopped

Cucumber slices, Crispy Parmesan Chips (page 122) or pepperoni chips (page 134)

In a large mixing bowl or food processor, combine the cream cheese, sour cream and ranch dressing. Blend well until the mixture is smooth. Add the garlic powder, onion powder and salt. Blend again.

Once the base is well mixed, add the Cheddar, jalapeños and bacon. Fold the dip together gently with a spatula. Cover the bowl and refrigerate until ready to serve. The dip will firm up the longer it sits in the fridge. Serve with cucumber slices or Parmesan or pepperoni chips!

cheaper than bottled ranch

Fresh herbs may be the best, but they can be expensive when not in season. This ranch dressing can be made for practically pennies at any time of year with dried herbs—herbs you probably already have in your pantry! I keep a jar with the pre-measured dry ingredients ready to go in my pantry. When I need more ranch, I simply add the wet ingredients to the jar, shake until well mixed and then store the jar in the fridge. This recipe is quick, frugal and delicious—and it has none of the high carbohydrate sugars and additives that many store-bought dressings contain.

Makes 10 ounces (295 ml)

1 tsp dried parsley
½ tsp garlic powder
½ tsp onion powder
¼ tsp dried dill
¼ tsp salt, plus more to taste
½ cup (120 ml) sour cream
½ cup (120 ml) mayo
1 tsp rice vinegar
1 tbsp (15 ml) water
Ground pepper

Combine the parsley, garlic powder, onion powder, dill and salt together in a 12-ounce (340-ml) jar with a lid. Add the sour cream, mayo, vinegar and water to the jar. Place the lid on the jar and shake until well combined. Season to taste with salt and pepper.

Refrigerate the dressing until ready to use. The flavors develop over time and I find this dressing is even better the next day. It will keep for 1 week in the fridge.

quick and simple alfredo sauce

Alfredo sauce is a delicious, naturally low-carb recipe. Unfortunately, some recipes call for flour to thicken up the sauce. This recipe substitutes cream cheese to add body back into the sauce. The garlic and Parmesan do an amazing job of adding flavor and salt and masking the tart that some people taste in cream cheese. This sauce is perfect on a bed of zucchini noodles, heart of palm noodles or simply as a topping on some shredded chicken. To make this an even more economical dish, add a few pieces of cooked cauliflower stalk that have been blended well. This is an optional addition that stretches the sauce a bit and also adds a bit of body.

Serves 6 ⬅

¼ cup (57 g) butter

2 cloves garlic, finely chopped

1 cup (240 ml) heavy cream

4 oz (113 g) cream cheese

¼–½ cup (61–122 g) cooked and blended cauliflower stalks (optional)

½ cup (50 g) grated Parmesan cheese

Salt and ground pepper

In a small saucepan over medium-low heat, combine the butter and garlic. Stir the garlic to keep it from burning. After the garlic has softened, about 3 minutes, turn the heat to low or simmer.

Add the heavy cream, cream cheese and blended cauliflower (if using). Continue to stir the sauce on low until it is smooth and well combined. Add the Parmesan cheese and stir slowly until it has melted into the sauce, 3 to 5 minutes. The Parmesan will add salt to the dish so taste for saltiness at the very end of cooking, once the sauce is finished and the Parmesan has melted into it.

I enjoy a smooth sauce, so once cooled I blend the Alfredo sauce in a blender or food processor. If you enjoy the tiny chunks of garlic in your Alfredo sauce, then skip this step. Season to taste with salt and pepper.

ballpark nacho cheese sauce

This recipe for cheese sauce is delicious as a dip for seasoned pork rinds or spooned over roasted vegetables. I don't care how old I am, I will never not have a place in my heart for cheese sauce.

Serves 8 ⬅

1 cup (240 ml) heavy cream
4 oz (113 g) cream cheese
1 (8-oz [226-g]) block of Cheddar cheese, shredded
¼ tsp onion powder
¼ tsp salt, plus more if needed
¼ cup (60 ml) chicken stock
½ tsp xanthan gum
Ground pepper

Add the heavy cream in a medium saucepan over medium-low heat. Add the cream cheese and stir with a wooden spoon, breaking up the cream cheese as you go. Once well combined, lower the heat to a simmer and add the Cheddar cheese. Continue to stir slowly until the cheese has melted into the sauce. Add the onion powder and salt and stir to combine.

There is a slight variation in cheeses based on the brand that you use. The cheese sauce may be extremely thick. Thin it out with chicken stock, 1 to 2 tablespoons (15 to 30 ml) at a time until the sauce reaches your desired consistency. Turn off the heat and whisk in the xanthan gum. Continue to whisk for about 1 minute until the sauce is smooth. This sauce will thicken further as it cools. Season to taste with salt and pepper, and store any leftover sauce in the refrigerator.

does-it-all spinach dip

Frozen spinach is an affordable Keto-friendly staple. I always have a bag or two on hand in my freezer. This recipe for creamy spinach dip is a total crowd-pleaser. It's also one of the most versatile recipes for a side. You can add more cream or chicken stock to thin the dip out into a delicious creamed spinach. Or try baking it with a bit more Parmesan cheese on top for a wonderful cheesy spinach casserole. I serve it as a dip with Crispy Parmesan Chips (page 122). If I'm serving as a creamed spinach, I enjoy it alongside Lemon-Pepper Whole Roast Chicken (page 14).

Serves 6 ⬅

1 (16-oz [454-g]) bag of frozen spinach, thawed and drained

4 oz (113 g) cream cheese

1 cup (113 g) shredded white Cheddar cheese

½ cup (120 ml) heavy cream

¼ tsp garlic powder

¼ tsp salt

¼ cup (25 g) Parmesan cheese, plus more for garnish

½ cup (120 ml) sour cream (optional)

Place the frozen spinach in a medium, microwave-safe bowl. Microwave for 3 to 5 minutes until thawed. Pile the spinach onto paper towels, a kitchen towel or cheesecloth. Wring out as much water as possible. Set aside.

In a medium saucepan over low heat, combine the cream cheese, Cheddar cheese, heavy cream and garlic powder. Stir gently until the cheese is melted into the cream sauce. Add the spinach and stir until well incorporated. Add the salt, Parmesan cheese and the sour cream (if using) for a creamier dip.

guacamole with pepperoni chips

Avocados are a delicious, creamy, healthy, fat-packed addition to the Ketogenic diet. I love them on their own, but whipped into a guacamole is pretty hard to beat. Although tortilla chips are a natural fit for a nice side of guac, the carb count is just too high to make them worth the splurge. Crispy, baked pepperoni chips are the perfect low-carb accompaniment to this delicious guacamole dip.

Serves 4 ←

Pepperoni Chips
1 (6-oz [170-g]) bag of pepperoni

Guacamole
2–4 ripe avocados
2 tbsp (30 ml) lime juice
¼ tsp garlic powder
¼ tsp onion powder
¼ tsp salt
¼ tsp chili powder
¼ tsp cayenne pepper (optional)

Preheat the oven to 350°F (177°C, or gas mark 4). Line a baking sheet with parchment paper.

To make the pepperoni chips: Spread the pepperoni slices over the entire surface of the baking sheet and place it in the oven for 5 minutes. Remove the baking sheet from the oven and dab excess oil off of the baking sheet with a paper towel. Turn the pepperoni and bake for 3 to 5 minutes until crisp. Remove the pepperoni and allow it to dry on a paper towel.

To make the guacamole: Combine the avocados, lime juice, garlic powder, onion powder, salt, chili powder and cayenne (if using) in a large mixing bowl. Using a spatula or wooden spoon, mix the ingredients together while smashing the avocado against the side of the bowl. Keep mashing the avocado pieces until you have reached your desired texture; if you prefer a chunkier guacamole this will take less time.

Use the pepperoni in place of chips to enjoy your guacamole. To re-crisp, place the pepperoni on a paper towel–lined plate and microwave for 15 seconds.

"use it or lose it" leftover land

Never be bored with leftovers again. As much as I hate wasting food, I also hate eating the same thing day after day after day. The idea behind this chapter was developing recipes that had creative new uses for many ingredients you probably have in your fridge. Have a steak you're not sure what to do with? Use it in my Philly Cheesesteak Skillet (page 138). This chapter is full of recipes that really come in handy when you're searching for something fun to do with a fridge full of leftovers.

philly cheesesteak skillet

Steak is one of the trickiest things to reheat well. A perfectly cooked steak, once chilled in the fridge, is easy to overcook when reheating. It's also an expensive ingredient and one of the meals that I'm always looking for new ways to prepare. Letting a steak go to waste is something that does not happen in my home. Utilizing leftover steak in a Philly cheesesteak skillet is one of the quickest, easiest dinners around and a perfect way to make sure that leftover steak is just as good as its first go-around.

Serves 2 ←

1–2 tbsp (15–30 ml) cooking oil, divided
1 small onion, thinly sliced
1 bell pepper, sliced (optional)
2 tbsp (30 ml) beef stock or broth
1 lb (454 g) any type of cooked steak, thinly sliced
Sliced or shredded provolone

In a medium cast-iron skillet, heat 1 tablespoon (15 ml) of oil over medium heat and add the onion. Sauté for 5 to 10 minutes until the onion has softened and browned. Remove the onion. If you're using the bell pepper, add the remaining 1 tablespoon (15 ml) of cooking oil and the pepper. Cook for 5 to 10 minutes until you achieve your preferred level of doneness.

Turn off the heat and add the cooked onion back in. Stir the onion and pepper together and spread them out along the surface of the pan. Add the stock, steak and provolone cheese. Place the skillet under the broiler for 8 minutes, watching carefully. When the cheese has bubbled and browned, remove the skillet from the oven. Divide this among 2 plates and enjoy immediately.

italian sub-less salad

A Keto grocery favorite is deli meat: roast beef, roast turkey, different types of bologna and salami are all usually great Keto options. When you can't pile them in a giant sub and enjoy them like you used to, you can use this clever recipe that re-creates all the flavors of that sub sandwich in a Keto-friendly salad. Roll up a variety of deli meats and cut them into pinwheels for an upscale plating option—or just stack and slice! The vinaigrette used in this recipe is even better after sitting in the fridge for a day. Remember to remove it from the fridge about half an hour before serving because the olive oil tends to solidify in the fridge.

Serves 4 ◀

Dressing
½ cup (120 ml) red wine vinegar

1 tbsp (5 g) dried Italian seasoning

¼ tsp garlic powder

¼ tsp salt

¼ tsp ground pepper

⅓ cup (80 ml) light olive oil

Salad
Lettuce, any kind

Any Keto-friendly, no-sugar-added deli meats (roast beef, turkey, bologna, salami and pepperoni)

Olives (optional)

Banana peppers (optional)

Shredded Parmesan cheese (optional)

To make the dressing: In a medium-sized mixing bowl, combine the vinegar, Italian seasoning, garlic powder, salt and pepper. Whisk to mix. While whisking, slowly drizzle in the oil.

To make the salad: Place the lettuce in a serving bowl or 4 salad bowls. Deli meat can be rolled up in any combination and sliced for pinwheels, or simply stacked and then sliced. Add the deli meat on top of the lettuce. Add the olives, peppers and Parmesan (if using). Pour one-quarter of the dressing over the salad.

Keep the unused portion of the Italian vinaigrette in the refrigerator. The dressing will keep in the fridge for up to 1 week.

easy cheesy chicken quesadillas

Sometimes when you go low carb, you end up using a knife and fork, a lot. Ordering things without the bread means that you end up missing out on a lot of holdable foods. I miss the convenience of finger foods. Combine this with never wanting to waste a single ounce of food and you have the inspiration behind this recipe. Instead of a carb-loaded traditional tortilla, this recipe uses cheese in a skillet, which crisps up beautifully and makes this Keto quesadilla a very convenient finger food.

Serves 2 ⬅

4 oz (113 g) shredded Cheddar cheese, divided

8 oz (226 g) leftover, cooked chicken breast

1 tbsp (15 ml) sour cream, plus more for serving

¼ tsp taco seasoning

Guacamole (page 134)

Pico de gallo or salsa (optional)

Melt 3 ounces (85 g) of Cheddar cheese in a nonstick skillet. Over medium heat, brown the cheese until it is a golden-brown crispy shell, about 5 minutes.

In a separate bowl, shred the chicken and stir in the sour cream, taco seasoning and remaining cheese. Add the chicken mixture to half of the crispy cheese shell and fold the empty side over the chicken. Reduce the heat to low and allow the center to warm for 1 minute. Flip the quesadilla to the other side and allow it to warm for 1 minute. Remove the quesadilla from the pan and allow it to drain on a paper towel for 1 minute.

Cut and serve with sour cream and guacamole, plus pico de gallo or salsa (if using) for dipping.

dough-stretching desserts

Often people are afraid that going Keto means having to give up desserts. Have no fear! With a few simple swaps you can turn most desserts into delicious, low-carb treats. This chapter is full of easy-on-the-wallet, easy-on-the-carb favorites. Some Keto recipes require special ingredients usually available only online. These recipes contain ingredients that you can find only at your local grocery store. Serve the Simple Chocolate Pots de Crème (page 152) to guests at a dinner party and no one will even know they are enjoying a Ketogenic treat. Set out some Lemon Loaf (page 156) for afternoon tea or enjoy Maple Pecan Shortbread Bars (page 160) at any time. The Saturday Morning Chocolate Donuts (page 147) are a perfect, portable treat for busy days.

saturday morning chocolate donuts

This recipe is called Saturday Morning Chocolate Donuts because this is always what Saturday mornings meant to me. Whether it was an after-sports treat as a child or even as a weekend reward as an adult, chocolate-covered donuts have always held a special place in my heart. Like anything else I crave, I developed this delicious recipe to re-create those old favorites using Keto-friendly ingredients. These donuts are rich and chocolatey—and the coating seals in the moisture which means that they actually store well! Enjoy these donuts anytime, not just on Saturday mornings.

Makes 6 donuts ⇐

Donuts
2 eggs
2 oz (57 g) cream cheese
¼ cup (60 ml) sour cream
⅓ cup (40 g) powdered sweetener
1 tsp vanilla extract
⅔ cup (69 g) almond flour
⅔ cup (59 g) unsweetened cocoa powder
¼ cup (28 g) coconut flour
1 tsp baking powder

Glaze
1 tbsp (14 g) coconut oil
1 oz (28 g) sugar-free chocolate
1 tbsp (12 g) powdered sweetener

Preheat the oven to 350°F (177°C, or gas mark 4). Have a 6-well donut pan ready.

To make the donuts: Combine the eggs, cream cheese, sour cream, sweetener and vanilla in a food processor. Pulse all the ingredients until smooth. In a medium mixing bowl, combine the almond flour, cocoa powder, coconut flour and baking powder. Whisk the dry ingredients together and then add them to the mixture in the food processor.

Pulse for a few seconds and then remove the lid, scrape the sides down, replace the lid and pulse for a few seconds more. The batter will be thick. Place the batter in a piping bag or in a large ziplock bag. If using a plastic bag, cut the end to make a ¾-inch (2-cm) opening. Pipe the batter into the wells of the donut pan. Distribute the batter equally between the 6 donut wells.

Bake for 8 to 10 minutes until the donuts feel set. Allow them to cool completely before removing the donuts from the pan.

To make the glaze: Melt together the coconut oil, sugar-free chocolate and the sweetener. Stir the ingredients together until well combined. After the donuts have cooled, remove them from the donut pan and place them upside down on a serving platter. Top each with a spoonful of the glaze. Allow the glaze to set at room temperature for about 10 minutes before serving. Refrigerate any leftovers in an airtight container.

no bake 5-minute peanut butter mousse

I love to bake. I really, really love to bake. Sometimes, however, I crave something sweet and simple and easy to assemble. This mousse comes together in about five minutes and is just so effortless. Pipe the mousse into a clear glass for an elegant presentation, or simply divide it into two bowls and get ready to dig in. This recipe is a great way to quickly satisfy a chocolate craving or sweet tooth attack—it's sure to please.

Serves 2 ⬅

8 oz (226 g) cream cheese

1 cup (240 ml) heavy whipping cream

½ cup (96 g) sweetener

¼ cup (22 g) unsweetened cocoa powder

2 tbsp (32 g) low-carb peanut butter

1 tsp vanilla extract

Combine the cream cheese, heavy whipping cream, sweetener, cocoa powder, peanut butter and vanilla in a medium mixing bowl. Whip the mousse together with a hand mixer on the lowest speed for 3 to 5 minutes until it reaches a smooth consistency.

Scrape around the sides of the mixing bowl with a spatula to make sure there are no larger pieces of cream cheese that haven't blended into the mousse.

Spoon the mousse into serving dishes. This can be served immediately. Refrigerate any leftovers.

save the airfare key lime tart

Key lime pie is one of my favorite desserts on earth! Most Keto recipes for key lime pie call for homemade Keto condensed milk. This is an expensive and time-consuming ingredient to make. The day I decided I would attempt a Keto key lime pie, I came up with a recipe that is both simple and frugal. While I can't bring myself to call this key lime pie, this tart sure does satisfy the craving.

Serves 8 ←

Crust
1 cup (104 g) almond flour
½ cup (56 g) coconut flour
¼ cup (48 g) sweetener
3 tbsp (45 ml) melted butter

Filling
8 oz (226 g) cream cheese
4 eggs
¼ cup (60 ml) fresh lime juice
¼ cup (48 g) sweetener
4 egg yolks
¼ cup (60 ml) heavy cream
1 tsp lime zest

Preheat the oven to 325°F (163°C, or gas mark 3) and place a rack at the bottom.

To make the crust: In a medium bowl, combine the almond flour, coconut flour, sweetener and melted butter until well mixed and crumbly. Press the mixture into the bottom of an 8 x 8–inch (20 x 20–cm) tart pan, pie pan or baking dish. Prebake the crust for 8 to 10 minutes. The crust should be set and a light golden brown.

To make the filling: Blend the cream cheese, eggs, lime juice, sweetener, egg yolks and heavy cream together in a blender or with a hand mixer. Stir the lime zest in last to keep the threads intact.

To make the tart: Pour the mixture over the prebaked crust. Place the tart in the oven and add a piece of foil to the rack above the pie pan to keep the tart from browning up too fast. Bake for 20 to 25 minutes. The tart will be ready when you can give the pan a bit of a shake and the filling seems set.

Allow the tart to cool before chilling it in the refrigerator. This tart is best served when chilled for at least 1 hour.

simple chocolate pots de crème

These rich and delicious chocolate pots are an absolutely decadent treat. They are also baked up individually in small ramekins for built-in portion control! You'll be baking these delicious chocolate pots in a water bath. If it sounds too daunting, you can bake the ramekins on a baking sheet. The effort is well worth it, however, resulting in a rich and silky texture throughout. Topped with whipped cream, this dessert is a total crowd-pleaser.

Makes 4 pots de crème ←

1½ cups (360 ml) heavy cream
½ cup (120 ml) half-and-half
1 tsp vanilla extract
4 egg yolks
½ cup (96 g) sweetener
1 (4-oz [113-g]) bar unsweetened baking chocolate, broken into small pieces
Sweetened whipped cream, for serving
Chocolate shavings, for serving

Preheat the oven to 350°F (177°C, or gas mark 4) and place a rack at the bottom.

In a large saucepot, combine the heavy cream, half-and-half, vanilla, egg yolks and sweetener. Whisk the ingredients together. Turn the heat to simmer and add the baking chocolate. Stir the mixture for 5 to 10 minutes until the chocolate has completely melted into the cream.

Pour the pot de crème mixture into four 4-ounce (113-g) ramekins. Place the ramekins in a baking dish and pour warm water into the dish. The water should be level with the chocolate in the ramekins. Place the baking dish in the oven and bake for 30 to 40 minutes until set.

Enjoy with some sweetened whipped cream and extra chocolate shavings for a garnish.

top the coffee shop pumpkin bread

I love the flavors of fall, rich and warm and cinnamon-filled. I do not, however, love the incredibly high carb counts of many of the coffee shop pumpkin treats that are available. I developed this recipe to satisfy the cravings of fall without having to go off my Ketogenic diet. This bread is amazing served with hot tea or coffee.

Serves 12 ⬅

Pumpkin Bread
6 eggs

1 cup (258 g) almond butter

½ cup (96 g) sweetener

1 cup (244 g) pumpkin puree

1 tsp cinnamon

1 tbsp (6 g) pumpkin pie spice

1 tsp vanilla extract

1 tbsp (15 ml) melted butter

Glaze
1 oz (28 g) cream cheese

2 tbsp (28 g) butter

2 tbsp (30 ml) heavy cream

1 tbsp (12 g) sweetener

Few drops of vanilla extract

Preheat the oven to 350°F (177°C, or gas mark 4). Line a loaf pan with parchment paper.

To make the bread: Combine the eggs, almond butter, sweetener, pumpkin puree, cinnamon, pumpkin pie spice, vanilla and butter in a food processor or medium mixing bowl. Blend until smooth. Pour the batter into the loaf pan. Bake for 30 minutes, or until set.

To make the glaze: Combine the cream cheese, butter, heavy cream, sweetener and vanilla in a small saucepan. Cook over low heat until creamy and smooth. Stir while simmering for 3 to 4 minutes to thicken the glaze. Turn the heat off and allow the glaze to cool while the pumpkin loaf is cooking.

Once the loaf comes out of the oven, allow it to cool for 5 to 10 minutes before pouring the glaze over it. Pour the glaze right over the loaf while it's still in the pan. Allow it to cool for 30 minutes before slicing into 1-inch (2.5-cm) servings.

lemon loaf

These lemon loaf slices are a great low-carb alternative to the sugary coffee shop version, an old favorite of mine. A great treat for afternoon coffee or tea, or for an anytime dessert. This recipe will be sure to satisfy your sweet tooth. The glaze hardens nicely and allows this loaf to travel well when packed in a lunch.

Serves 12

Loaf
2 eggs
¼ cup (57 g) butter, melted
2 oz (57 g) cream cheese
¼ cup (60 ml) sour cream
¾ cup (144 g) sweetener
¼ cup (60 ml) lemon juice
6 oz (170 g) almond flour
1 tbsp (14 g) baking powder

Glaze
2 tbsp (28 g) butter
2 tbsp (30 ml) heavy cream
2 tbsp (30 ml) lemon juice
2 tbsp (24 g) sweetener
Lemon zest (optional)

Preheat the oven to 350°F (177°C, or gas mark 4). Line a loaf pan with parchment paper.

To make the loaf: Combine the eggs, butter, cream cheese, sour cream, sweetener and lemon juice in a food processor. Blend until smooth. In a separate bowl, combine the almond flour and baking powder. Stir the dry ingredients together and then fold them into the wet mixture. Pour the batter into the loaf pan and bake for 30 minutes in the preheated oven.

While the lemon loaf bakes, make the glaze. In a small saucepan, combine the butter, cream, lemon juice, sweetener and lemon zest (if using). Heat over low for about 5 minutes until well combined and slightly thickened. Set the glaze aside until the lemon loaf is baked.

Once you remove the loaf from the oven, pour the glaze over the cake while still in the loaf pan. Allow the loaf to cool for 10 to 15 minutes and then place it in the fridge for at least 1 hour. This loaf is best served chilled.

cinnamon pecan coffee cake

I love classic coffee cake. It's a great breakfast or afternoon tea treat. The crumbly topping was always my favorite part. Usually made from sugar, butter and flour, it's certainly not an option for a Keto menu. This recipe re-creates the flavors and texture of a traditional coffee cake with only a few simple ingredient swaps.

Serves 12 ←

Coffee Cake

¼ cup (57 g) butter, softened

4 eggs

2 oz (57 g) cream cheese

¼ cup (60 ml) sour cream

½ cup (96 g) sweetener

1 tbsp (15 ml) vanilla extract

½ tsp cinnamon

2 cups (208 g) almond flour

½ tsp xanthan gum

1 tsp baking powder

Topping

½ cup (55 g) pecans

1 tbsp (14 g) butter

2 tbsp (24 g) sweetener

2 tbsp (13 g) almond flour

Preheat the oven to 350°F (177°C, or gas mark 4).

To make the coffee cake: In a medium mixing bowl, combine the butter, eggs and cream cheese. Blend them together with a hand mixer or in a stand mixer. Add the sour cream, sweetener, vanilla and cinnamon and blend together until smooth, about 2 minutes. In a separate bowl, combine the almond flour, xanthan gum and baking powder. Fold the dry ingredients into the wet ingredients.

To make the topping: Combine the pecans, butter, sweetener and almond flour in a food processor. Pulse until the mixture is crumbly.

Spoon the batter into a nonstick 8 x 8–inch (20 x 20–cm) pan. Sprinkle the topping over the cake and bake, uncovered, for about 30 minutes until set. Allow the cake to cool for at least 10 minutes before slicing.

maple pecan shortbread bars

Serves 12 ⬅

A perfect fall coffee accompaniment: This dessert is not too sweet, but has a nice balanced shortbread taste and texture. You can double the glaze for a thicker, sweeter topping. Add bacon if you really want to take it up a notch.

Shortbread

½ cup (114 g) butter

2 eggs

½ cup (96 g) sweetener

½ tsp maple extract

½ tsp vanilla extract

2 cups (208 g) almond flour

½ cup (55 g) pecans

¼ tsp xanthan gum

½ tsp baking powder

Glaze

½ cup (120 ml) heavy cream

¼ cup (57 g) butter

2 tbsp (24 g) sweetener

½ tsp maple extract

¼ tsp vanilla extract

For Topping (optional)

½ cup (55 g) chopped pecans

Preheat the oven to 325°F (163°C, or gas mark 3) and place a rack at the bottom. Line a 9 x 13–inch (23 x 33–cm) baking dish with parchment paper.

Mix together the butter, eggs, sweetener, maple extract and vanilla in a stand mixer, food processor or in a bowl with a hand mixer.

In a separate bowl, combine the almond flour, pecans, xanthan gum and baking powder. Add the almond flour mixture to the egg mixture. Stir to combine. Pour the mixture into the baking dish and press it down with wet fingers. Make sure it is spread evenly in the dish. Bake for 40 to 45 minutes.

While the shortbread bakes, make the glaze. In a small saucepan, combine the cream, butter, sweetener, maple extract and vanilla. Stir the mixture over low heat until well incorporated. Allow it to simmer on low for 10 minutes, stirring frequently as the glaze thickens.

Once the shortbread is finished baking, remove it from the oven and allow it to cool for 10 minutes before pouring the glaze over the top. Top with additional pecans if desired. Allow the shortbread to cool for at least 1 hour before slicing into bars and serving. Chilling it in the fridge will allow the glaze to set even quicker.

does-it-all yellow cake

There is no reason to miss out on anything when you adopt a Ketogenic diet. I searched and searched for a great basic yellow cake recipe. Some were delicious, but they didn't quite hit the mark. This recipe for a does-it-all yellow vanilla cake can be baked up in cake pans or as cupcakes. It slices well for cake decorating and rises just enough to make a beautiful surface for piping icing onto cupcakes. This cake recipe really does do it all.

Serves 12

4 egg whites
2 oz (57 g) cream cheese
4 egg yolks
¼ cup (48 g) sweetener
¼ cup (60 ml) sour cream
1 tbsp (15 ml) vanilla extract
6 oz (170 g) almond flour
1 tbsp (14 g) baking powder
Keto frosting of choice, for serving

Preheat the oven to 350°F (177°C, or gas mark 4).

Whip the egg whites into stiff peaks, about 5 minutes. Set aside.

Combine the cream cheese, egg yolks, sweetener, sour cream and vanilla in a food processor. Process until well incorporated.

In a separate bowl, stir the almond flour and the baking powder together. Add the dry ingredients to the wet ingredients. Pulse until combined. Fold in the egg whites.

Pour the cake batter into a round cake pan and bake for 30 to 40 minutes, depending on the size. You can also make this batter into 12 cupcakes. Bake them for 20 to 25 minutes until a toothpick comes out clean. Top with your favorite Keto frosting and serve.

➜ acknowledgments ⬅

Thank you to everyone who encouraged me to follow my passion. To those who told me I could when I wasn't so sure. To my mother, who never misses an opportunity to let me know she's proud of me. To Autumn, whose unwavering enthusiasm and friendship and support ushered me through this last year. To Amy, Susan, Lisa, Bethany and Cynthia, the women who carried me and held me when I needed it most. To Aimee and Shannon, the sisters I never had but somehow found. To Lisa, my photographer, thank you for your energy, commitment and creativity. To Heather, I am forever grateful for our friendship. To Lisa and Ariel, my young ones, I love you both. To my Barnaby, thank you for being my puppy. You're the best friend a girl could ask for. And a giant thanks to the thousands of people I have met online, who have taken a moment of their time to send kind words, encouragement and support. You'll never know what a difference you have made in my life. Finally, to Jenna, your kindness, patience and humor made this process an absolute joy.

➜ about the author ⬅

Emily has been cooking and baking since childhood, and her love of food inspired her to start her own dessert catering company. She also fought a lifelong battle with her weight and tried every diet out there until she found the Ketogenic diet. Her success on the Keto diet led her to start her food blog, KetoCopy.com.

Emily enjoys transforming traditional recipes into creative Ketogenic versions. Her passion is to share her recipes, advice and tutorials aimed at helping people learn how to adopt a Ketogenic lifestyle. Emily is a lifelong resident of Ann Arbor, Michigan.

→ index ←